What Sort of Doctor?

Assessing Quality of Care in General Practice

Royal College of General Practitioners

Published by

The Royal College of General Practitioners

ISBN 85084104 6

July 1985

The Royal College of General Practitioners

The Royal College of General Practitioners was founded in 1952, with this object:

"To encourage, foster, and maintain the highest possible standards in general medical practice and for that purpose to take or join with others in taking steps consistent with the charitable nature of that object which may assist towards the same."

Among its responsibilities under its Royal Charter the College is entitled to:

"Encourage the publication by general medical practitioners of research into medical or scientific subjects with a view to the improvement of general medical practice in any field and to undertake or assist others in undertaking such research.

Diffuse information on all matters affecting general medical practice and establish, print, publish, issue and circulate such papers, journals, magazines, books, periodicals, and publications and hold such meetings, conferences, seminars, and instructional courses as may assist the object of the College."

College Headquarters

The headquarters of the Royal College is at 14 Princes Gate, Hyde Park, London SW7 1PU (Telephone: 01-581 3232). Enquiries should be addressed to the General Administrator.

Exeter Publications Office

Reports from General Practice are published by the Exeter Publications Office of the College, 9 Marlborough Road, Exeter EX2 4TJ (Telephone 0392 57938).

Acknowledgement

The Editor thanks Stuart Pharmaceuticals Ltd for financial help in publishing this *Report from General Practice*.

Contents

First Working Party
(1980–1981)

Chairman

J. A. R. Lawson, OBE, FRCGP
General Practitioner, Dundee

Members

J. C. Hasler, OBE, MD, FRCGP
General Practitioner,
Sonning Common

M. L. Marinker, MD, FRCGP
Director, MSD Foundation

Lotte T. Newman, BSc, FRCGP
General Practitioner, London

J. S. Norell, FRCGP
General Practitioner, London

D. A. Pendleton, DPhil, ABPsS
Stuart Fellow,
Royal College of General Practitioners

J. H. Walker, MD, FRCGP, FFCM
Professor of Family and Community Medicine,
University of Newcastle upon Tyne

Second Working Party
(1982–1984)

Chairman

T. P. C. Schofield, MA, FRCGP, MRCP
General Practitioner, Shipston on Stour

Members

J. Emmanuel, MRCGP
General Practitioner,
Bexhill on Sea

J. M. Forrest, MRCGP
General Practitioner, Liverpool

L. Henderson, MBE, FRCPEd, FRCGP
General Practitioner,
Grantown-on-Spey

J. P. Horder, CBE, MA, FRCP, FRCPEd,
FRCGP, FRCPsych
Visiting Fellow,
King's Fund College

J. Lee, MSc, FRCGP
General Practitioner, London

A. J. Membrey, FRCGP
General Practitioner,
Tunbridge Wells

K. Mourin, MA, FRCGP
General Practitioner,
Dereham, Norfolk

J. S. Norell, FRCGP
General Practitioner, London

D. A. Pendleton, DPhil, ABPsS
Stuart Fellow,
Royal College of General Practitioners

M. Ryan, MRCGP, MFCM
General Practitioner,
Livingston, Scotland

J. Woodward, MRCGP
General Practitioner,
Sidcup, Kent

Foreword

I AM delighted to have been invited to introduce this publication. During my many years of working for the College, nothing has given me greater satisfaction than being a member of the first "What Sort of Doctor?" working party. This view has also been expressed to me by other members of the group. The working party was exploring new ground in its task of devising a method of assessment relevant to all general practitioners in their own practices. This was a tremendous challenge. The first working party, when presenting its report, was aware that it had merely pointed the way in indicating the possible application of practice-based assessment and stating that more research into method was required. This task was assumed by the second working party, which, during a two-year period, was engaged in testing this method of performance review.

This publication will, I am sure, be of interest to all members of the College, to many general practitioners who are not members, and to others who have an interest in assessment procedures. It is about quality of care and its measurement, which concerns all in the medical profession and also all our patients.

J. A. R. LAWSON
President
Royal College of General Practitioners

Timetable

What Sort of Doctor?

INTRODUCTION

IN September 1980 the Board of Censors of the Royal College of General Practitioners set up a working party to devise "a method of assessing the performance of established general practitioners in the setting of their own practices." A report was issued 12 months later under the title "What Sort of Doctor?", the main text being published in the November 1981 issue of the *Journal of the Royal College of General Practitioners*.

The following year, a second working party began the further exploration of the ideas contained in the report. The present document consolidates the experiences and findings of the two groups and suggests directions for future developments.

Throughout the document we have used the male gender when describing doctors. This is solely to avoid frequent repetition of 'he or she' and 'his or her' and in no way diminishes our recognition of the equal contribution that women doctors make to the profession.

BACKGROUND

Several factors combined to produce the stimulus which eventually led to the setting up of the first working party. Foremost among these was concern that there should be a reliable way of judging the quality of the service offered to patients by the individual general practitioner. The absence of accepted standards for the many facets of his everyday work was painfully obvious; so too was the lack of agreement on the core content. General practice had gradually emerged from its traditional isolation, but the cherished individualism of general practitioners had preserved a situation in which each doctor virtually wrote his own job description. The opening up of general practice, the sharing of ideas and exposing different ways of practising, was something which touched only a small minority of doctors.

Historically, the Balint seminars of the early 1950s constituted the first methodical study of part of the general practitioner's work (Balint, 1968); its focus was the doctor-patient relationship developed "in the intimacy of the consulting room" when, in Sir James Spence's classical description, "a person who is ill or believes himself to be ill seeks the advice of a doctor whom he trusts" (Spence, 1960). Later, a number of College publications, including *The Field of Work of the Family Doctor* (Gillie Report, 1963) and *The Future General Practitioner* (RCGP, 1972), mapped out the potentially enormous territory of general practice, but no method existed for systematically studying how this challenge was actually being met, for looking at the general practitioner's performance in its total perspective. This provided another incentive for exploring the idea of practice-based assessment. Among others, its possible uses were:

- As an additional mode of entry to College membership, independent of the MRCGP examination

- In the appraisal of potential fellows of the College
- For the purpose of the re-accreditation of members.

FIRST WORKING PARTY

It was against this background that the first working party approached the task of devising a method of assessment that would be relevant to general practitioners, as well as being practical, acceptable, adaptable and testable. Between them, the seven members (five of whom were in active practice) brought a long experience of family medicine, work in Balint groups, involvement in medical education at all levels, intimate knowledge of the MRCGP examination, and active participation in trainer selection procedures. This wealth of experience proved invaluable in the ensuing discussions at which ideas were pooled, compared and questioned. As methods of assessment were thought up, they were tried out among members of the working party and subjected to a sequence of testing, reformulating and refining.

Hitherto, the conventional approach had been to assemble the basic ingredients of knowledge, skills and attitudes deemed necessary for a doctor's work and then to draw up assessment techniques appropriate to each of these elements. But it was precisely this procedure which had been found wanting when applied to the complex nature of general practice and which had stimulated the search for a more satisfactory alternative.

A new approach

The working party decided to tackle the problem in a totally different way, going back to first principles and focusing primarily on the general practitioner rather than on general practice. What were the attributes that really mattered? Which qualities would he or she need to possess in order to discharge adequately the diverse and formidable obligations of a general practitioner in today's society? This decision was crucial and proved extraordinarily productive.

At this stage the working party was deliberately postponing any consideration of the feasibility, or indeed, the possibility, of assessing such attributes. (Considerations like these had led to standard assessment techniques concentrating on examinable items which, while not of the greatest relevance, were at least 'safe' and scientifically objective.) It resolved first to try to determine precisely which were the most important features for obtaining the measure of a colleague in general practice. These would not then be discarded for want of available assessment techniques. If they were truly important then some form of test procedures would have to be devised; and if these lacked 'scientific objectivity', then it would have to be so.

It will be apparent that the working party was already bringing to its task a pragmatism characteristic of general practice, as well as a sound theoretical base. In particular, it was prepared to grasp the nettle of making value judgements about vital features of general practice before attempting to create measurements in mathematically precise terms, confident that these would nevertheless be understood by all experienced practitioners.

✳ Areas of performance *See appendix I*

Reviewing the wide range of responsibilities which general practitioners undertake today, explicitly or by implication, the working party selected the following areas to encompass the desirable attributes. These divisions overlap to some extent but were found to be capable of separate assessment. Collectively, they were felt to reflect the multiple dimensions of a general practitioner's life and work.

1. *Clinical competence:* the technical aspects of the doctor's work; what would commonly be understood as 'medical'.

2. *Accessibility:* the ease with which the community of patients has access to the practice and to the facilities within it; the doctor's own availability.

3. *Ability to communicate:* the doctor's receptivity; getting on to the wavelength of his patients, whatever their background; accurately conveying his thoughts to practice staff and to colleagues within the practice and outside.

Despite the comprehensiveness, something seemed to be missing: an attribute not easy to define but which would provide the crucial underpinning. The working party later added:

4. *Professional values:* the doctor's perception of his role in relation to individual patients and to the practice community; his ideals and sense of priorities; the spirit which motivates and guides him in the gradual evolution of his practice.

For each of these four areas, a statement was drawn up summarizing the essential nature of the attributes in question. In doing this the working party tried to avoid being impossibly idealistic or boringly banal.
The statements are reproduced below:

1. Professional values

(a) The doctor tries to render a personal service which is comprehensive and continuing.

(b) In his practice arrangements he balances his own convenience against that of his patients, takes into account his responsibility to the wider practice community, and is mindful of the interests of society at large.

(c) He accepts the obligation to maintain his own mental and physical health.

(d) He puts a high value on communication skills.

(e) He subjects his work to critical self-scrutiny and peer review, and accepts a commitment to improve his skills and widen his range of services in response to newly disclosed needs.

(f) He recognizes that researching one's own discipline and teaching others are part of one's own professional obligations.

(g) He sees that part of his professional role is to bring about a measure of independence: he encourages self-help and keeps in bounds his own need to be needed.

(h) His clinical decisions reflect the true long-term interests of his patients.

(i) He is careful to preserve confidentiality.

2. Accessibility

(a) The doctor is broadly accessible to the satisfaction of his practice population.

(b) He can be seen quickly for urgent matters, and normally within two days for non-urgent matters.

(c) He is prepared to visit patients in their homes.

(d) He is available for advice on the telephone at known times.

(e) His staff are helpful to patients and see themselves as facilitating the doctor-patient contact.

(f) He provides adequate out-of-hours cover.

(g) His patients are aware of the procedure by which the doctor or his deputy can be contacted at any time of the day or night.

3. Clinical competence

(a) The doctor is shrewd, observant, and skilled at eliciting relevant information.

(b) He works swiftly but surely without undue sense of rush.

(c) In general, his history-taking and physical examinations are economical, and his notes pithy and informative; but when occasion demands, he is capable of more exhaustive procedures.

(d) His personal style of consulting is consistent but is responsive to individual patients' needs and demonstrates a logical problem-defining process.

(e) He links physical, social and emotional factors when formulating his assessment of the patient and when planning further management.

(f) He makes appropriate use of other members of the practice's health care team, and of colleagues and agencies outside.

(g) He prescribes effectively, with caution and mindful of costs.

(h) He carefully follows up his patient and actively seeks to learn the consequences of his action or inaction.

(i) The clinical records he keeps help him to monitor patients' progress and to plan anticipatory care and other preventive measures.

(j) He employs opportunistic health education and constantly reinforces advice on lifestyles; and by giving relevant information freely to patients tries to encourage them to share responsibility for their own health care.

4. *Ability to communicate*

(a) The doctor is receptive, and conveys a sense of attentiveness, of professional concern for the patient's unfolding problem, and of personal commitment to the patient.

(b) He shares information and decision-making with the patient as much as possible; the patient feels supported and encouraged by the doctor, and better informed than before, and so feels more capable of handling future episodes of a similar illness.

(c) Notices and educational displays in the waiting room are clear, and as far as possible positive and optimistic.

(d) The staff handle enquiries sensitively.

(e) Entries in the clinical records are legible, ordered, pertinent, accurate and retrievable.

(f) They are capable of being used for teaching, research and audit.

(g) Letters to consultants are informative and explicit about the reason for referral and the doctor's expectations.

(h) The ancillary staff and other members of the practice's health care team have frequent opportunity to meet the doctors informally to discuss aspects of practice policy or matters of mutual clinical interest.

(i) Times are set aside for more formal meetings when longer-term issues can be discussed.

(j) The doctor is sensitive to the views of the staff and anxious to bring them into his policy-making as far as possible.

These statements were amended very slightly by the second working party (Appendix 1).

Criteria

The next step was to determine sets of criteria against which these attributes could be assessed. The criteria eventually emerged as paired statements, polarizing doctor behaviour as admirable or reprehensible and features of the practice as desirable or unacceptable (Appendix 2). For example, under 'Accessibility' the statement: "The ancillary staff facilitate doctor-patient contacts in the most helpful way" is paired with: "The staff are over-protective of the doctor and make it very difficult for patients to have access to him." Under 'Professional values': "He believes in the importance of continuity of care, gives a personal service, and tries to make it as comprehensive as possible" is paired with: "He does not think continuity of care matters, delegates excessively, and his clinical interests are dominated by one or two hobby-horses."

In formulating these criteria the working party were aware of walking a tightrope between vague, platitudinous statements and precisely demarcated, quantitative ones. The resulting compromise produced criteria which were fairly explicit but not so precise as to permit rating merely by reference to a check-list. The assessment procedure deliberately left room for the exercise of judgement by informed and experienced colleagues.

Sources of information

It was now necessary to devise ways of searching for the numerous criteria. Drawing on experience of the MRCGP examination, the procedures of regional committees in selecting trainers, and the techniques employed by the Joint Committee on Postgraduate Training for General Practice, the working party assembled a large battery of possible methods. Some were discarded because they overlapped with others which did the job better, or because their yield was unacceptably low. Eventually, six sources of information were chosen on the basis of being relevant, feasible, highly informative, and complementary.

1. *The practice profile:* a comprehensive questionnaire completed by the doctor and recording the salient features of the practice (Appendix 3).

2. *Direct observation* of the practice and its functioning under ordinary working conditions.

3. *Discussion* with ancillary staff, paramedical members of the health team, and the doctor's partners.

4. *Inspection* of the practice's registers and indexes, and randomly selected clinical records.

5. *Review* of recently video-taped consultations, together with the relevant records, to be made with the doctor.

6. *Interviewing* the doctor semi-formally on a wide range of topics concerned with patient care and practice development.

To help those making the assessments, specific questions were drawn up relating to the various criteria being looked at by the test method. These were later incorporated by the second working party in a fuller description of each of the procedures.

Each method of assessment produces information about all four areas of the doctor's performance. This information can be recorded on a grid (Appendix 4), which provides not just a description of the doctor's practice and his style of work but a profile of his strengths and weaknesses as judged by the assessors. It is then possible to use the paired statements for each criterion and to record a judgement about the doctor's level of performance, or degree of achievement of each criterion, on a four-point scale, as follows:

> 3 Totally
> 2 Moderately
> 1 Minimally
> 0 Not at all

Presenting findings in this way can serve two distinct purposes. It allows the quality of the practitioner's performance to be judged against levels previously agreed: a regulatory function. More important, in the view of the working party, is the educational function achieved by feeding back the assessment findings to the practitioner concerned, enabling him to appreciate how he and his practice are seen by his peers and following which he may take whatever remedial steps he deems appropriate. The voluntary nature of this exposure to scrutiny by peers is implicit throughout, and recognition of the doctor's autonomy was a major consideration.

In the final section of its report the first working party noted matters which required further study:

1. *Technical aspects:* concerning reliability, sampling, logistics, standards, and correlation with other assessment techniques.

2. *Organization:* including how assessors were to be trained, and the role of the College's faculties.

3. *Applications of the assessment tool:* especially as a means of improving the quality of general practitioners' continuing education.

Reactions

The publication of the first report created considerable interest both within and outside the profession, and not a little admiration for what was seen as a significant advance on previous attempts to tackle the problem of measuring quality of care in general practice. It also aroused some negative reactions, including:

- Scepticism about feasibility, logistics, individual motivation, and the allocation of College resources.

- Disdain for the concept of 'backdoor' entry to membership of the College: the notion that admission could be by any means other than the current rigorous, reproducible and academically authenticated examination.

- Anxiety that the existence of a relevant and workable assessment tool might encourage outside bodies to attempt to judge the quality of current general practice and then influence the direction it should take.

The general feeling, however, was that the ideas contained in the report were promising and deserved to be further researched and developed.

SECOND WORKING PARTY

A second working party was set up in September 1982 to test this method of performance review under field conditions, in order to gauge its feasibility and wider acceptability. Two of its members had served on the first working party. It decided to concentrate on developing the educational potential of the method rather than its use as a regulatory mechanism, because the reliability of the method had not then been established nor acceptable levels of performance agreed. It endorsed the principle of peer review, defined as assessment by peers against agreed criteria of good practice.

The new working party began, as its predecessor had done, by testing out the proposed procedures on its own members in a series of reciprocal assessment visits. Following this, it redefined the terminology of the original report as follows:

- 'Areas' or 'Attributes' became 'Areas of performance'

- 'Assessment methods' became 'Sources of information'

- 'Criteria' described discrete and definable elements of agreed good practice

- 'Level of performance' denoted the degree or frequency with which each element was achieved or performed.

Three additional criteria were included:

- 'Punctuality' was included in the area of 'Accessibility'

- 'Preventive medicine' and 'Care of emergencies' were given separate prominence in the area of 'Clinical competence'.

Field trials

The main task now was to test the acceptability and feasibility of these proposals as a method of reviewing the performance of general practitioners in their own practices. It was decided to make use of the faculty structure of the College and to invite three faculties, Merseyside, South East Thames and South East Scotland, to assist the working party in this next phase of development and evaluation of the project. A study day would be held in each faculty for interested doctors, at which the proposals would be explained and any anxieties or doubts explored. It was hoped that agreement would be reached on plans for a series of practice visits. After these visits had taken place there would be a second meeting at which the experience of visiting could be discussed. This sequence has been completed in South East Thames and Merseyside and the evaluation report below is based on their findings. Only an initial meeting has been held in South East Scotland.

The different rates of progress reflect the way the project was organized in the respective faculties. In South East Thames and Merseyside responsibility was undertaken by one individual with the assistance of a small working group, while in South East Scotland it was the responsibility of the faculty board and its officers. The original study days in the first two faculties lasted nearly a whole day, and at the end the large majority of doctors felt adequately prepared to become involved in visits. In South East Scotland an evening meeting was held; possibly this did not allow adequate time for anxieties to be allayed and commitments made.

The immediate problem facing the two faculties conducting the visits was how the participants were to acquire sufficient experience to act as assessors. In South East Thames five geographical groups were formed with six to eight doctors in each group, one doctor acting as co-ordinator. The initial visits in each group were made by teams which included an experienced assessor from the working party. Ideally each doctor in the group should have three involvements: (a) being visited, (b) being a junior visitor, and (c) being a senior visitor. In the event, it was not always possible to observe this sequence.

On Merseyside a group of five practitioners initially visited each other and then, as a second phase, they became the co-ordinators of five similar sized groups.

As an additional method of conveying information about the procedure to be followed on the assessment visits, comprehensive notes were issued by the working party, and separate sets were sent to the practitioners being visited as well as to those acting as assessors (Appendix 5, Appendix 6).

Evaluation

Evaluation was supervised by the College's Stuart Fellow who was a member of both working parties and who had played a prominent role in the preliminary briefing of interested doctors. The working party went to great lengths to obtain adequate feedback, both from the assessors and the doctors who were subjects of the visits.

1. To help evaluate inter-observer reliability, each of the pair of assessors individually rated, on a four-point scale, the level of achievement noted for each criterion.

2. Assessors completed a questionnaire on the procedure followed.

3. To measure the validity of the assessment programme as a whole, doctors who had been visited rated the importance they attached to the individual criteria as elements of good practice. These doctors were also asked to return a questionnaire eliciting their views on:

   (a) the thoroughness and fairness of the visit
   (b) its value to them and their practices, and whether they expected anything to change as a result of the visit
   (c) the reaction of their partners and staff
   (d) ways in which the visit might have been better.

   Some months later each doctor was asked what changes had occurred in the practice as a result of the visit.

Finally, it was intended that the participants would meet again on completion of the programme of visits to review their individual experiences and to give collective feedback to the working party. Most of them did so at a meeting held in February 1984.

Results

From the admittedly limited documentation available for more than 35 assessment visits, and the experience of reciprocal visits carried out by members of both working parties, it is possible to come to some tentative conclusions.

1. *Validity of the criteria*
With the exceptions of 'professionalism' and ' personal behaviour', the criteria were considered to be appropriate by nearly all the assessors. Difficulties were encountered in the assessment of some criteria listed under 'clinical competence', and to a lesser extent with 'self-awareness' and 'personal behaviour'. The doctors who had been assessed also confirmed the validity of the criteria, except 'teaching and research', which many thought inappropriate.

2. *Acceptability of the method*
No reservations were expressed either by the assessors or by those assessed; in particular, no-one found the procedure threatening.

3. *Sources of information used by the assessors*
Some were thought to be more valuable than others, but they were generally approved. Video recordings of the consultations were considered by many to produce the most valuable information, but also created occasional technical difficulties and problems over the selection of cases to be assessed.

4. *Reliability of the ratings*
Discrepancies in the criteria ratings were low; each criterion could therefore be regarded as reliable.*

5. *Value of the visits*
Many doctors said that the visit and the subsequent report were a valuable stimulus to change in their practices. Several doctors, however, expressed disappointment that the report they received about themselves and their practices had been insufficiently critical and had not revealed anything they did not already know. The assessors' understandable concern to be complimentary and non-threatening in the interests of preserving good relations among professional, and occasionally neighbouring, colleagues had sometimes resulted in a report which lacked insight and incisiveness and thus detracted from its value. Enquiries three months later showed that where specific comments had been made in the reports these were acknowledged and very often acted upon, a few doctors acquiring new equipment or introducing changes in the way their practices were run (Appendix 7). Influence on clinical behaviour was not so easy to discern.

So far as the doctors who had been assessed were concerned, a mere description of the practice did not seem to be enough: what they looked for was a critique, a reasoned judgement on their merit as general practitioners. The assessors, on the other hand, all expressed great enthusiasm for the procedure and said how valuable it was to them. They felt privileged to be allowed to intrude into a colleague's practice, and had received valuable insights into the different ways the challenge of being a responsible and responsive practitioner could be met.

On the whole, all the experience which has accumulated in the three years since the original publication of "What Sort of Doctor?" has vindicated the innovatory ideas of the first working party. Some modifications have been made to the procedures and there is undoubtedly room for further improvement; but the areas chosen have been confirmed as the right ones, the criteria are valid, and the detailed procedure for the assessment visit itself has proved acceptable to all concerned.

Both faculties reported that the exercise had provided an incentive for involving members in faculty activities. A further group of doctors in each of the faculties has asked to be included in a second programme of visiting. In South East Thames, the original group has requested that the visits should be repeated in two years' time, with at least one of the visitors from the first visit, so that comparisons could be made and progress or lack of it could be demonstrated. In Merseyside there was also interest in developing the method further, particularly in looking more closely at the care provided for specific groups of patients and at other aspects of practice management.

---

* Reliability should be tested statistically. The problem here, however, is that each doctor was visited by a different pair of judges, so most tests of reliability would normally assess only the judges rather than the scales. It was decided, therefore, to use Cohen's *Kappa* (Cohen, 1960) across the judges, and to disregard the uniqueness of each pair. This produces a particularly severe test of reliability, and Cohen's measure is already a conservative test. By this means it was possible to demonstrate reliability at the .05 probability level or better for over half of the scales, on what was effectively each pair's only visit. This reliability, already at a surprisingly high level, might reasonably be expected to be improved on subsequent visits, or by a small amount of training. Unreliable scales might also be amended by using this method.

The involvement of faculties was essential if the method was to undergo genuine field trials as had been planned. While the exercise was initiated from the centre and continues to be monitored there, the local planning, organization and execution was firmly in the hands of faculty members. Another very welcome feature is the involvement of a number of non-members.

UNRESOLVED ISSUES

In the course of further refining the assessment procedures many complex questions will have to be faced. We list the major issues below.

More or fewer criteria?

If a few criteria were found eventually to correlate very closely with a large number of others, it would be possible to cut down on the total number. On the other hand, additional relevant criteria might be introduced. 'Punctuality' was one such. Conceivably, 'sense of humour' might come to be regarded as a *sine qua non* for the contemporary general practitioner struggling to be all things to all men and women.

Clearly, lists of criteria cannot be regarded as fixed for all time, but should they at least be fixed for all places at any one time? This is a controversial question. In different settings, no doubt different emphasis will be placed on the various criteria. It seems that it is the required level of performance which is most likely to vary from place to place and time to time, there being little prospect at present of agreement on a universal standard of performance in general practice.

Whose criteria?

It may be thought that the practitioners carrying out the assessment visits had the various criteria imposed on them, and that they might have done better if each group had chosen its own. But the criteria listed in our protocol were not plucked out of the air in some arbitrary fashion. They were originally selected by the first working party on the basis of long experience, serious thought and intensive testing. Furthermore, the criteria are being offered to assessors as a working tool, and with the explicit invitation to submit them to critical examination by working with them, so that they can be modified if necessary. The fact that scarcely any modifications have so far been suggested by the many participants may be taken as an indication of the true relevance, and possibly, universality, of the present set of criteria.

Judging the practice or the practitioner?

This has proved a recurring problem, and for good reason. A general practitioner does not merely work from his practice: in very many ways the practice and its arrangements represent the sort of doctor he is. That is why our assessment procedure relies so heavily on information about the practice itself. Nowadays, only a minority are in single-handed practice; most practitioners are in partnerships or practise with colleagues from a health centre. Many features of 'the practice' therefore result from a blend of separate influences, and in these circumstances it is not always easy for assessors to determine precisely what should be attributed to the individual doctor; nor, except in the consultation itself, accurately to judge his personal merit. Nevertheless, assessors strive to get the measure of the doctor himself and try to avoid this crucial assessment being diluted by factors which are clearly matters of 'cabinet responsibility'.

Strengths and weaknesses

Assessors were repeatedly cautioned to set out the strengths of the doctor and his practice before embarking on any criticisms. The reason for this was not only to produce a more comprehensive, rounded view of what was discovered but to provide encouragement to maintain and to develop those particular strengths. Though not intended as a way of sugaring the pill, some doctors at the receiving end expressed irritation at the recital of descriptive features of which they were perfectly well aware, and would have preferred comment to be confined to those areas where remedial action was called for. In terms of a medical analogy, what they wanted was a diagnostic report, rather than the descriptive account required for life assurance purposes.

The following extract, from an actual report of an assessment visit carried out by two members of the first working party, illustrates one approach.

"The video-taped consultations revealed the doctor as thoughtful and considerate with patients, having a friendly, informal style, prepared to let patients tell their story in their own way, and preferring to keep an open mind about the true nature of the problem. Urine investigations were often called on. Recourse was frequently had to antibiotic therapy, despite the tentative nature of the diagnosis. Explanations were offered to the patient, but explicit instructions were rarely given. Usually, attention was confined to the matter in hand; anticipatory care was not observed in the five consultations we witnessed, in one at least of which there was a clear opportunity to do so. The doctor's approach was unhurried, the consultations extending beyond the budgeted five minutes in many cases. Approval was voiced for patients' self-help attempts. There was appropriate use of the nurse."

In many of the reports the assessors' criticisms were muted, and this was especially marked in the area of 'Clinical competence'. In part, this was due to the intrinsic difficulty of making judgements on the basis of relatively slender evidence (often including no more than four video-taped consultations); in part, to deference to his colleague who was after all 'in the driving seat'. The feedback to the working party strongly suggests, however, that doctors being assessed would welcome more pointed criticism. It could be argued that it is preferable in this sort of procedure that a few practitioners should be asking for more criticism, rather than many asking for less or complaining that strengths were not noticed.

Comments or recommendations?

A related question is whether assessors ought to make precise recommendations when they encounter what they judge as practice deficiencies or inadequate performance on the part of the doctor. Or should they merely record these features and perhaps comment on their implications, leaving it to the doctor himself to take the action he deems necessary? While the latter approach might be thought to show more respect for the doctor's autonomy, and possibly for his intelligence, again we have to record the strong desire by those criticized for specific advice on how to bring about improvements in the service they are offering. It has to be accepted that some practitioners may be genuinely at a loss over what practical steps to take to improve matters. Moreover, the obligation to give sound advice can act as a deterrent to glib criticism.

There are few, if any, activities in general practice for which a single right way has been identified with certainty, and this is why the criteria listed by the working party are less explicit than they might have been. In the present state of our knowledge it must usually be left to the individual practitioner to determine his priorities. What the assessor tries to do is to elicit whether the doctor has given thought to the issues and is aware of the compromises he has made and of their implications.

Attainment or development?

In the course of visiting doctors in their practices what very often impressed the assessors most was not the evidence of solid achievement but signs of purposeful struggle. No two practices are precisely alike and comparisons between the attainments of different general practitioners, even neighbours, can be rendered virtually meaningless by the existence or otherwise of certain factors; for example, partners' attitudes, attachment of paramedical staff, the proximity and adequacy of hospital facilities, and perhaps most important of all, the habits and expectations of the practice population. Some of our colleagues practise under relatively favourable conditions; others are sadly disadvantaged. But irrespective of the surrounding circumstances, a crucial determinant in the assessment of "What Sort of Doctor?" is the evidence of professional growth and the development of the practice in response to patients' emerging needs.

For this reason it has been suggested that having a single assessment is of less value to a doctor than a pair of such visits separated by an interval of two or three years. This approach would certainly be in line with the concept that the vital comparison is not between one doctor and another, but between the same doctor before and after. Some sort of external reality check is of course important, and the sharing of ideas and experiences remains an integral part of such assessments. But the true outcome of this kind of continuing education must be sought in the way the doctor and his practice actually develop over time.

Peer review or consumers' verdict?

Commentators have pointed out the lack of involvement of patients in our procedures, and it has been suggested that they could have been included as a source of information about the quality of the service offered them, or even as visiting assessors. The omission may be considered the more surprising in the current atmosphere of consumerism and with the steady growth of patient participation groups in general practice. The second working party did in fact seriously consider soliciting the opinion of the practice's patients but concluded that this was not feasible. Furthermore it would have detracted from the status of the assessment as a peer review conducted by fellow professionals and based entirely upon their interpretations.

It could be argued that we have already gone outside by talking to ancillary staff, nurses and health visitors; and it is true that discussion with them does give valuable insights into the nature of the practice. However, their views are sought primarily on aspects of the service they themselves are providing, and on their relationships with other members of the practice team.

Nevertheless, patients do have something to say about vital aspects of the provision of care and could be involved in discussing criteria for good quality care. They may not be competent to judge its overall quality, but they do know, for instance, whether their views have been taken into consideration and whether they have been treated like human beings. At present, doctors themselves make these judgements; in future a more prominent place may be found for the patient's voice.

Quis custodiet custodes?

In the problematical area of trying to assess a colleague's work fairly, there is no doubt about the effectiveness of learning through doing. Here, at least, there is no substitute for experience. However, the assessment of clinical competence is clearly revealed as the weak spot in our procedure and thought has been given to ways in which assessors might gain greater proficiency in that area; for example, through special training in the analysis of video-taped consultations. As in the assessment visit itself, it is essential that the consulting doctor's own comments are available during the discussion in order to avoid an element of voyeurism being introduced, and to enable the assessors to gain insight into a consultation at which they were not actually present.

The wider question remains: how are sufficient numbers of competent assessors to be fielded? There is no short cut to the steady progression outlined earlier. Ideally, the first step is for the potential assessor himself to be assessed, preferably by colleagues already well versed in the procedure. After this he may join a pair of assessors as an observer and obtain a different slant on the process. Then he may be ready to act as an assessor himself, initially accompanying a much more experienced colleague.

The problem of logistics could be formidable, especially if a centrally organized, special team of assessors were to be maintained. A more attractive alternative would be to encourage faculty-based assessments, as described in this report, because this would help to spread the load; it would also be totally in keeping with the principle of mutual learning. The role of the College centrally would then be to offer advice and help as required, to monitor the results of the assessment visits, and to make available individual members to act as external assessors from time to time. This should be sufficient to ensure that there is not a drift away from reasonably comparable methods of assessment and accepted levels of performance, while at the same time allowing that circumstances may alter cases.

Medical science and the art of general practice

Here we enter an area steeped in controversy. We find ourselves caught in crossfire: from some traditionalists for whom 'the art of general practice' expresses important ineffable, intuitive, unmeasurable and undescribable aspects of their endeavours; and from the academically orientated who are pinning their hope on 'scientific objectivity' to improve the prestige of general practice and to secure for it its rightful place among the other medical disciplines.

The traditionalists believe that the practice of family medicine does not lend itself to methods of systematic and critical assessment, and that attempts to define quality in general practice, let alone measure it, are doomed to failure. Many academics, on the other hand, have expressed disappointment that the College should be seen to encourage the development of an assessment procedure which employs such 'unscientific' means as value judgements and subjective impressions, which so clearly lacks the mathematical precision of the existing and highly acclaimed MRCGP examination, and whose approach is as far from conventional academic wisdom as it is possible to get.

We have argued earlier that to have confined ourselves to those features which could be 'proved' or lend themselves to precise measurement would have robbed our assessment procedure of any possibility of looking at a number of subtle and highly valued aspects of general practice. We felt justified in relying for 'proof' on acceptance by experienced colleagues, on the test of common sense, and on the evidence of subsequent outcome. We asked: "Does it feel right?" and "Does it work?"

General practitioners are capable of making complex judgements and of being used as sensitive measuring instruments. Using peer judgement as the basis for assessing performance can be quite scientific so long as it is reliable. The smallness of the samples usually available to the assessors must induce caution in making generalizations about the doctor and his practice, but the assessment procedure can claim to be soundly based since many different sources of information are being used and a wide range of activities and attributes looked at. In effect, those making the judgements are seeking common messages from these several sources of information. We cannot believe it wise that in its quest for academic respectability general practice should avoid considering manifestly important aspects of its discipline merely because these do not readily lend themselves to appraisal by the methods of conventional medical science.

A similar point of view has been put forward by Alvan Feinstein (1983) who believes that the best way to restore and preserve clinical art is to make the art more scientific. He offers 'clinimetric science' as "an additional clinical investigation that can augment the scientific basis of clinical practice, while re-humanizing the contents of research data and restoring analytic emphasis to the art of patient care". The purpose is to "enable physicians (and patients) to become masters rather than slaves of the technology by expanding it to include human data, by aiming at human goals, and by making it respond to human aspirations".

It may well be that there is still much about our everyday work which cannot be precisely quantified and which, for the present at least, is more suitably regarded as 'the art of general practice'. But as it happens, in the field of Art valid judgements can be made, and it may be instructive to consider how these are arrived at. In his dissertation, *On Quality in Art*, Jakob Rosenberg (1969) quotes from an aesthetician:

> "The artistically sensitive and trained observer will be able to recognize and appraise it with great assurance when he is in its presence."

And from a literary critic:

> "Value cannot be demonstrated except through the communication of what is valuable. Critical principles, in fact, need wary handling. They can never be a substitute for discernment, though they may assist to avoid unnecessary blunders."

Rosenberg summarized his own position as follows:

> "Artistic value or quality in a work of art is not merely a matter of personal opinion but to a high degree also a matter of common agreement among artistically sensitive and trained observers ... Quality may be sensed in a work of art without a proper approach and analysis, but it cannot be fully experienced without these means and without a thorough and definite effort on the part of the observer."

We came to very similar conclusions in formulating the procedures for judging the quality of the general practitioner's performance.

1. Experienced general practitioners are able to reach agreement on matters of quality, criteria, and levels of performance.

2. The process of assessment depends entirely on free and whole-hearted communication; "value cannot be demonstrated except through the communication of what is valuable."

3. Proper assessment relies on the efforts of sensitive and trained observers who are capable of applying criteria reliably and with discernment.

4. Their judgements must be based on pertinent observation, and they must be able to explain clearly how their conclusions are derived.

This approach is not only thoroughly professional but, we would claim, conforms to sound scientific principles.

POSSIBLE APPLICATIONS

The arrival on the scene of a tool originally designed for one purpose may prompt consideration of other possible uses for it. Apart from its role in continuing education, the further ways in which studies of individual practitioner performance could be used are considered below. Some may be thought to be distinct possibilities, others to be speculative at this stage.

What sort of member?

At present, College members are not called upon to demonstrate their continued competence as general practitioners in order to retain their membership status. That status is assured by passing a once-and-for-all entry examination. The counterparts of our College in some other countries do possess re-accreditation procedures.

These are based mainly on educational criteria and involve written examinations, listing the postgraduate courses attended, and totalling the number of hours spent annually reading medical journals and textbooks. A practice-based assessment could offer a much more direct method of measuring the practitioner's performance for the purpose of re-accreditation.

What sort of fellow?

Fellowship of the College is an award conferred in recognition of a member's contribution to general practice, judged largely on repute. It has been argued that a more searching appraisal of the doctor's way of practising should supplement the traditional lines of enquiry. Clearly, there ought to be something distinguished about fellows, and perhaps their behaviour as practitioners should be seen to be not merely adequate but exemplary: literally, a good example. If this were accepted, then the standards applied when assessing potential fellows, that is, the level of performance required of them, could be raised accordingly in the course of the assessment visit.

What sort of trainer?

It is only comparatively recently that serious attention has been given to the trainer's competence as a doctor. The usual sources of information for this were necessarily indirect, as may be judged from the fact that hospital consultants and the local postgraduate clinical tutor were among those to whom assessors might have recourse. As a consequence, trainer selection relied more on noting practice facilities and arrangements, and the trainer's grasp of educational principles and his use of them. It is now recognized that trainees inevitably to some extent model their behaviour on what they observe in their trainers; and if for no other reason, this makes it important that the trainer should serve as a good model and display a suitably high standard of performance as a practitioner. The procedures outlined in the first "What Sort of Doctor?" report lend themselves to trainer selection, and at least one region has already included them in its assessment of trainers (Schofield and Hasler, 1984).

What sort of vocational training?

The only attempts, to date, to evaluate the effectiveness of vocational training for general practice have relied on the techniques of the MRCGP examination to measure performance. Since it is unclear how closely examination marks correlate with subsequent behaviour as a principal in general practice, it would seem desirable – to say the least – to have a less remote method for studying the outcome of vocational training. This could be achieved by applying practice-based assessments to ex-trainees a year or two after they have become established as principals. With sufficient numbers it might eventually be possible to make regional comparisons, or even to compare the outcomes of training offered by different schemes.

What sort of practice manager?

Many of the staff in the practices visited were attracted to the idea of peer review and commented that they would like to have the opportunity of visiting other practices and of being similarly assessed themselves. A methodology comparable to that of "What Sort of Doctor?" could be used to develop criteria for good practice management and to promote practice-based assessment visits by practice managers as well as by other members of the team.

What sort of faculty?

Many faculties seem uncertain about their purpose and find it difficult to involve members and non-members in their activities. Reciprocal assessment visits would provide an excellent opportunity for achieving this. Discussing criteria for good practice, and review by peers to encourage the development of doctors and practices, would be evidence of a faculty working in a truly collegiate way to promote good quality care for patients.

To introduce innovations successfully, faculties will need a structure which can harness the enthusiasm of individual members. The College centrally will continue to be needed to provide encouragement, support, and facilities for sharing ideas and experiences between the various faculties.

What sort of family medicine?

Of all branches of medicine, general practice remains the most individualistic. However much general practitioners aim for comprehensiveness in the care they give, they are inevitably selective, consciously or unconsciously. Ways of practising are determined not only by patients' needs: they are strongly influenced by the doctor's flair, style and preferences, as well as by local custom – not to speak of ritual. Family planning, paediatric surveillance, marital counselling, hypertension screening, diabetic clinics, injecting steroids into shoulders and elbows – these and many other worthwhile activities are being undertaken in varying degrees by general practitioners; but no-one does them all.

By putting together the individual profiles obtained from practice-based assessments, it should be possible to replace the present reliance on conjecture and mythology by a more accurate picture of present day family medicine and of accepted good practice.

What sort of College?

Since 1968, practitioners wishing to become members of the College have had to pass a formal written and oral examination, which over the years has become more geared towards those undertaking their vocational training. Nowadays the overwhelming majority of candidates are about to complete or have recently completed such training. Longer established practitioners seem to fare less well in tests of this sort, and many principals are discouraged from sitting an examination which directly tests not clinical behaviour or the ability to run a practice but rather the infrastructure of medical behaviour: the knowledge, skills and attitudes (or such elements as lend themselves to assessment by examination methods) acquired in the course of the three-year training, only one of which is spent actually in general practice.

Growing concern, among members as well as from outside, that the College was possibly being unnecessarily deprived of the contribution which many of these highly experienced practitioners could make led to the suggestion that an assessment method more relevant to their achievements and to the qualities they possessed might make possible their admission to the College's ranks as full members.

At the same time, worries were expressed about a practice-based assessment being offered as a substitute examination. The two assessment procedures, however, test two very different things; and they can be expected to attract two different populations of candidates. The MRCGP examination, being a test of vocational training, speaks about promise, about potential. It does not and cannot make a judgement about the merit of the candidate as a practising doctor and established principal.

The assessment visit, on the other hand, is designed to do precisely that. It judges the doctor's competence as an active practitioner in the setting of the very practice where he works and which he has played a part in fashioning. He is judged on the way he actually discharges his responsibilities towards individual patients, towards the practice population, towards his partners and practice staff, towards his own profession, and towards himself. The assessment looks for shrewd judgements rather than cleverness, for the wisdom acquired from experience rather than factual knowledge. It seeks evidence of a thinking and considerate doctor, one who is thoughtful in both senses of the word. It is able to distinguish the practitioner who has retained his professional integrity and who has neither succumbed to cynicism nor been defeated; one who has maintained a sense of proportion and kept in bounds his need to be needed.

To summarize: the judgement employed during the assessment visit is about the actuality of present performance and past achievement. It asks what sort of doctor the practitioner is, not what sort of doctor he or she may turn out to be. It is therefore reserved for those who have had time and opportunity to place their knowledge, skills and attitudes at the disposal of their patients: literally, to put them into practice. Thus the assessment procedure we have been describing is as unsuitable for the very recent recruit to general practice as the MRCGP examination is proving to be for the longer established principal.

CONCLUSIONS

In this document we have described the development of a form of assessment which possesses a number of novel features.

1. It is practice based and assesses the doctor's performance under ordinary working conditions.
2. It is voluntary, and so relies entirely on openness, trust, tact and mutual respect.
3. It embodies the principles of peer review; it is conducted by colleagues of comparable standing and experience.
4. For this reason there is a notable absence of the adversarial element characteristic of conventional assessment procedures; the doctor being assessed is eager to know how informed and experienced colleagues see him.
5. The assessment is not necessarily orientated towards the question of pass/fail; nor does the assessor make a straight comparison with 'right' answers or with his own preferred way of working. He tries to judge how well the doctor is tackling his task, faced with certain challenges and possessing particular resources; how effective and efficient he is.
6. The assessor brings to such judgements a perspective and breadth of understanding entirely characteristic of his profession. It is not just knowledge of general practice that allows him to fill that role: it is the experience of being a general practitioner.
7. All those engaged in these exercises, the assessed as well as the assessors, realize they are taking part in mutual learning and also in research of a kind; activities which are essential for professional growth.

Taken together these features represent a unique approach towards the further development of general practice which could eventually result in the accurate mapping of our discipline. By establishing modes of accepted good practice, individual practitioners would be able to follow the example of colleagues whose work they most admired. If widely adopted, such procedures would constitute unmistakable evidence of the profession's serious intention to put its house in order and through its own efforts measure up to its considerable responsibilities.

Acknowledgements

It is obvious that this work could not have been undertaken without the willing co-operation of many practitioners, in a number of faculties, who agreed to be the subject of assessment visits and later to act as the assessors. They gave their time generously. We are also indebted to their partners and practice staff for their contributions and for tolerating the inevitable partial disruption of the practice.

The working parties were fortunate to have the extremely efficient help of successive secretaries: Veronica Gilbert, Judith Halliwell and Sue Smith. They were in attendance at the many meetings and produced and circulated the considerable documentation generated by our discussions.

A number of distinguished individuals, within our profession and outside, kindly commented on the preliminary results of our studies. We should particularly like to express our gratitude to Professor Avedis Donabedian for the very close interest he has taken in our work. He has examined our assessment procedure at first hand and made valuable comments on its relevance and likely impact. We felt further inspired by the importance he attached to our work.

We are grateful to Stuart Pharmaceuticals Ltd for their generous support of the Stuart Fellow, who has been closely associated with this work, and of this publication.

References

Balint M. (1968) *The Doctor, His Patient and the Illness.* 2nd edn. London, Oxford University Press.

Cohen J. (1960) *A Co-efficient of Agreement for Nominal Scales. Educational & Psychological Measurement* **20**, 37–46.

Feinstein A.R. (1983) *The Development of Clinimetrics. Annals of Internal Medicine* **99**, 843–8.

Gillie Report (1963) *The Field of Work of the Family Doctor.* Report of the Central Health Services Council. London, HMSO.

Pendleton D., Schofield T., Tate P. et al. (1984) *The Consultation, An Approach to Learning and Teaching.* London, Oxford University Press.

Rosenberg J. (1969) *On Quality in Art: Criteria of Excellence, Past and Present.* London, Phaidon Press.

Royal College of General Practitioners (1972) *The Future General Practitioner: Learning and Teaching.* London, British Medical Journal.

Royal College of General Practitioners (1981) What sort of doctor? *Journal of the Royal College of General Practitioners* **31**, 698–702.

Spence J. (1960) *The Purpose and Practice of Medicine.* London, Oxford University Press.

Schofield T.P.C. and Hasler J.C. (1984) Approval of trainers and training practices in the Oxford Region. *British Medical Journal* **288**, 538–40, 614–8, 688–9.

APPENDIX 1
Areas of performance

1. Professional values

(a) The doctor tries to render a personal service which is comprehensive and continuing.

(b) In his practice arrangements he balances his own convenience against that of his patients, takes into account his responsibility to the wider practice community, and is mindful of the interests of society at large.

(c) He accepts the obligation to maintain his own mental and physical health.

(d) He puts a high value on communication skills.

(e) He subjects his work to critical self-scrutiny and peer review, and accepts a commitment to improve his skills and widen his range of services in response to newly disclosed needs.

(f) He recognizes that researching his discipline and teaching others are part of his professional obligations.

(g) He sees that part of his professional role is to bring about a measure of independence: he encourages self-help and keeps in bounds his own need to be needed.

(h) His clinical decisions reflect the true long-term interests of his patients.

(i) He is careful to preserve confidentiality.

2. Accessibility

(a) He can be seen quickly for urgent matters, and normally within two days for non-urgent matters.

(b) He is prepared to visit patients in their homes.

(c) He is available for advice on the telephone at known times.

(d) His staff are helpful to patients and see themselves as facilitating the doctor-patient contact.

(e) He provides adequate out-of-hours cover.

(f) His patients are aware of the procedure by which the doctor or his deputy can be contacted at any time of the day or night.

3. Clinical competence

(a) The doctor is shrewd, observant, and skilled at eliciting relevant information.

(b) He works swiftly but surely, without undue sense of rush.

(c) In general, his history-taking and physical examinations are economical, and his notes pithy and informative; but when occasion demands, he is capable of more exhaustive procedures.

(d) His personal style of consulting is consistent but is responsive to individual patients' needs and demonstrates a logical problem-defining process.

(e) He links physical, social and emotional factors when formulating his assessment of the patient and when planning further management.

(f) He makes appropriate use of other members of the practice's health care team, and of colleagues and agencies outside.

(g) He prescribes effectively, with caution and mindful of costs.

(h) He carefully follows up his patients and actively seeks to learn the consequences of his action or inaction.

(i) The clinical records he keeps help him to monitor patients' progress and to plan anticipatory care and other preventive measures.

(j) He employs opportunistic health education and constantly reinforces advice on lifestyles; and by giving relevant information freely to patients tries to encourage them to share responsibility for their own health care.

4. Ability to communicate

(a) The doctor is receptive, and conveys a sense of attentiveness, of professional concern for the patient's unfolding problem, and of personal commitment to the patient.

(b) He shares information and decision-making with the patient as much as possible; the patient feels supported and encouraged by the doctor and better informed than before, and so feels more capable of handling future episodes of a similar illness.

(c) Notices and educational displays in the waiting room are clear, and as far as possible positive and optimistic.

(d) The staff handle enquiries sensitively.

(e) Entries in the clinical records are legible, ordered, pertinent, accurate and retrievable.

(f) They are capable of being used for teaching, research and audit.

(g) Letters to consultants are informative and explicit about the reason for referral and the doctor's expectations.

(h) The ancillary staff and other members of the practice's health care team have frequent opportunity to meet the doctors informally to discuss aspects of practice policy or matters of mutual clinical interest.

(i) Times are set aside for more formal meetings when longer-term issues can be discussed.

(j) The doctor is sensitive to the views of staff and anxious to involve them in policy-making as far as possible.

APPENDIX 2
Criteria for assessment

1. Professional values

Perception of role

The doctor sees himself as providing a service to his practice population, sharing with others responsibility for promoting, preserving and restoring the health of individual patients.

The doctor regards medical practice solely as a way of earning a living or of encountering interesting clinical material.

Responsibilities

He balances his own convenience against that of his patients, and keeps the interests of the wider community in mind.

He invariably puts his own convenience above the needs of his patients, and has no concern for his wider responsibility to society.

Personal care

He believes in the importance of continuity of care, gives a personal service, and tries to make it as comprehensive as possible.

He does not think continuity of care matters, delegates excessively, and his clinical interests are dominated by one or two hobby horses.

Development

The practice has continually evolved over the years in response to newly disclosed health care needs, and is continuing to do so.

The nature of his practice is static. He is not in touch with fresh developments within his own profession. He regards the development of his practice as finished.

Professional growth

He maintains and improves his skills, and continually widens his horizons. He maintains his clinical curiosity and at the same time feels involved with his patients' problems.

He allows intellectual atrophy to set in and practises in a narrow, disjointed, mechanistic way. He relates only superficially to his patients.

Self-awareness

He subjects his work to critical self-scrutiny and review by colleagues. He enjoys being a general practitioner and he accepts the obligation to maintain his own physical and mental health.

He is complacent about the quality of his work and sees no point in reviewing it. He never reflects on what he is trying to achieve. He has become cynical or defeated, or drives himself excessively.

Personal behaviour

He is of good repute and known for his integrity. He displays dignity in his personal behaviour and honourable dealing with his partners. He has good relationships with colleagues and staff.

In his personal and private life he is not a good model. He is not well regarded by his peers.

Teaching and research

He is interested in teaching and research and sees these activities as part and parcel of professional life.

He is antipathetic towards anything to do with the academic aspects of general practice and has no thought for those who will follow him in his profession.

Communication

He places high value on communication, and recognizes the importance of achieving a shared view of problems with patients. Patients are open with him, trusting his and his staff's discretion.

He does not see communication as a two-way process, and does not know or care whether he is getting through to patients. He is careless about confidentiality.

Patients' autonomy

He encourages patients' self-help, and keeps in bounds his need to be needed. His clinical decisions reflect the true long-term interests of his patients.

He allows the development of unwholesome dependence on himself or on psychotropic drugs.

Professionalism

He is a thorough professional: a thinking, questioning doctor.

He equates being a doctor with being a provider; he behaves as a grocer, or a bartender.

2. Accessibility
Consulting arrangements

The doctor can be seen very quickly by patients for urgent matters during normal working hours. Patients with non-urgent matters are normally seen by their doctor within two days.

The doctor cannot usually be seen quickly for urgent matters during normal working hours. Patients with non-urgent matters usually have to wait several days for an apointment to see their own doctor.

Home visits

The doctor is prepared to visit patients in their homes; clear arrangements exist for requests.

The doctor is very reluctant to do home visits; arrangements for requests are confusing, and difficult for patients.

Patients' queries

The doctor deals with patients' queries himself, or gives clear guidelines to his staff on how to deal with them.

The doctor avoids dealing with queries himself, nor does he give clear guidelines to his staff on how to deal with them.

Contactability

The doctor can be very readily contacted by his staff for advice.

The doctor is very difficult to contact for advice.

Out-of-hours cover

The doctor provides adequate out-of-hours cover; the arrangements are clearly known and acceptable to his patients. He personally takes a share in the rota duty.

The doctor provides inadequate out-of-hours cover. The arrangements are poorly understood by his patients. He does not share in the rota duty.

Access to staff

Access to ancillary and attached staff is easy and the arrangements are made clear to patients.

Access to staff is difficult; arrangements are poorly understood by patients.

Facilitation

The ancillary staff facilitate doctor-patient contacts in the most helpful way.

The ancillary staff are over-protective of the doctor and make it very difficult for patients to have access to him.

Punctuality

The doctor does not keep patients and staff waiting unnecessarily.

The doctor is regularly late for appointments.

3. Clinical competence
History-taking

The doctor consistently gives evidence of his ability to take a relevant history. He appears to be listening to what his patient says and is able to respond to the verbal and non-verbal cues which he is given. He constructs his questions logically and puts them clearly. He uses the medical record both to verify and to amplify the history.

The doctor persistently fails to elicit a relevant history. He gives evidence of not hearing what his patient is saying, or of actively preventing the patient from communicating. He does not follow up verbal and non-verbal clues, or he actively pursues irrelevant aspects of the patient's history. He fails to verify points in the history by reference to the medical record, or fails to use the medical record itself as a source of further information about past events.

14

Physical examination

The doctor consistently makes an appropriate physical examination based on the history. His examinations are skilled and carried out with obvious consideration for the patient; they are more often concerned with clinical problem-solving than with ritual behaviour.

The doctor fails to make an appropriate physical examination based on the history. His examinations are cursory and are in other ways technically inadequate. He makes so-called 'full physical examinations' which seem in no way part of the problem-solving approach.

Defining the problem

The doctor's definition of the patient's problem is clearly based on the evidence presented. He does not make a habit of naming a disease, where there are no reasonable criteria for such a diagnosis. He consistently relates physical, social and psychological factors.

The doctor's definition of the patient's problems, his 'diagnosis', is unsupported by the evidence that he has collected, or by a reasonable interpretation of the probabilities. In formulating these problems he persistently fails to relate physical, social and psychological factors.

Seeking further information

The doctor's search for further information is clearly rooted in the clinical work which precedes it, or can be supported by a reasonable interpretation of probabilities. He tries to understand how the patient sees the problem.

The doctor's search for further information by investigation cannot be supported either by the clinical work which precedes it, or by a statement of reasonable probabilities. He is not interested in how the patient sees the problem.

Use of resources

He refers appropriately to other members of the primary health care team and to the hospital services, including consultants. He makes appropriate use of diagnostic and treatment equipment which the practice possesses.

He either fails appropriately to refer the patient to other members of the primary health care team, or he does so inappropriately. Similarly, his referrals to hospital are either unsupported by the preceding clinical work, or fail to occur when they should. He fails to use the diagnostic and treatment equipment in the practice when appropriate.

Explanation to the patient

His explanations are informative and clearly expressed; where appropriate he explains the likely causes of the problems and likely course of coming events.

He fails adequately to explain his understanding of the patient's problems, including, where appropriate, the causes of the problems and the likely course of events.

Management

He involves the patient in decisions on management. He gives clear and concise advice about management, especially lifestyle, diet, work and drug therapy.

He does not involve the patient in decision making. He fails to give clear advice about management, especially lifestyle, diet, work and drug therapy.

Prescribing

His use of drugs is appropriate. He has a disciplined and logical approach.

His use of drugs is inappropriate. He gives no evidence of a disciplined approach.

Preventive medicine

He consistently gives evidence of a willingness and ability to give both opportunistic and anticipatory care.

He fails to give appropriate opportunistic or anticipatory care.

Continuing care

The doctor, wherever appropriate, demonstrates his ability to make plans for the adequate follow-up of the patient. He goes out of his way to take personal responsibility for the continuing care of the patient, and imparts a sense of that continuity to the patient when appropriate. He has a considered approach to the long-term management of chronic conditions.

The doctor persistently fails to make plans for the adequate follow-up of the patient. He gives scant evidence of taking personal responsibility for clinical problems, or for ensuring that the patient has a sense of continuing care, when this might be appropriate. He has an *ad hoc* approach to the long-term management of chronic conditions.

Care of emergencies

He makes adequate provision for the immediate care of emergencies which he may encounter in his practice.

He is unable to provide adequate care for emergencies which he may encounter in his practice.

4. Ability to communicate

Communication with the patient

The doctor creates a receptive and calm atmosphere in the consulting room, and the patient is encouraged to communicate freely. He communicates his interest in the patient and his story. He actively explores the patient's view of the problem, and seeks to achieve a high degree of agreement between it and his own view of the problem. He gives evidence of his own commitment to the patient now and in the future. There is clear and adequate information on the services provided by the practice. The doctor's communication with his patient helps him to define the reasons for the patient's attendance at the surgery, to manage the patient's problems, to educate the patient on relevant health care matters, to offer support to the patient and to promote health in its broadest sense.

The doctor's lack of communication with his patient hinders him from defining the reasons for the patient's attendance at the surgery, managing the patient's problems, educating his patient on relevant health care matters, offering support to his patient or promoting health in its broadest sense. He fails to create a receptive and calm atmosphere in the consulting room, such that the patient may be encouraged to communicate freely. There is inadequate information on the services provided by the practice.

Communication with ancillary staff

There are frequent opportunities for informal meetings, and written communications are clear and concise. There is evidence of negotiated practice policies about such matters as the handling of requests for repeat prescriptions, home visits and urgently required consultations. The doctor shows overall concern for the welfare of his staff.

There is little evidence of communication with the staff. He provides no guidelines for handling such matters as requests for repeat prescriptions, home visits, and urgently required consultation. He shows little or no concern for the welfare of his staff.

Communication with colleagues and other members of the health care team

Regular meetings take place. The doctor shows sensitivity to the problems encountered by his colleagues and an understanding of the respective roles of each member of the team. The doctor encourages a free exchange of ideas between all those involved in the provision of health care in the practice.

The doctor discourages communication between members of the health care team. He is insensitive to their problems and shows no understanding of their various roles.

Referral letters

Usually the doctor's letters are typewritten and copies are kept on file. The letters are succinct, giving a clear summary of the relevant evidence and a statement of the doctor's formulation of the problem. The consultant is clearly informed about the general practitioner's expectations of the consultation requested. The letters convey a vivid thumb-nail sketch of the patient as a person.

The doctor's letters are not usually typewritten, nor are copies kept in the patient's file. They do not clearly summarize the relevant evidence, nor do they clearly state problems. The doctor's expectations of help from the consultant are rarely made explicit. The letters persistently fail to refer to the patient as a unique individual in a particular social context.

Clinical records

The practice records are complete and accurate in regard to basic data. All entries in the records are legible and entered sequentially. Notes of each consultation or visit are made in such a way as to convey the key features. Hospital reports, laboratory and x-ray reports are filed in date order and show evidence of having been 'pruned'. The clinical records are capable of use in decision-making, teaching, research and audit.

The doctor's records give incomplete or inaccurate basic data. The clinical notes are illegible and are not entered sequentially. The reader cannot clearly and quickly summarize the key features of past consultations. The accompanying letters, hospital reports and laboratory reports are not in date order and show no evidence of having been 'pruned'. The records cannot easily be used for decision-making, teaching, research or audit.

APPENDIX 3
Practice profile

Name _____

Address _____

_____

_____

1. Practice list size _____
2. Your status in the practice: Principal _____
   Assistant _____
3. Length of experience in general practice _____
4. Number of years in present practice _____
5. Personal posts held outside the practice:

_____

_____

_____

The practice

6. Type of practice:

   Dispensing _____ Rural _____
   Teaching _____ Urban _____
   Mixed _____

7. Total number of doctors in the practice (providing general medical services):
   Full-time partners _____
   Part-time partners _____
   Assistants _____
   Trainees _____
   Your personal list size _____
   Average list size per principal in the practice _____
   Average list size per principal in the FPC area _____
   Percentage of patients over 65 years of age _____
   Percentage of patients under 5 years of age _____

8. Please describe the main geographical, social and environmental features of the practice, including any local health problems:

_____

_____

_____

Access

9. Is there an appointments system? _____
10. What is the normal booking rate? _____
11. How many appointments are available each week (excluding special clinics) in the practice?

_____

12. What hours is your building open on a weekday?

_____

13. How do patients contact a doctor out of hours?

_____

_____

_____

14. How do patients contact a doctor in an emergency during the day?

_____

_____

_____

15. How do receptionists contact a doctor in an emergency during the day?

_____

_____

_____

16. What proportion of your out-of-hours work is done by:
    the partnership only? _____
    a larger rota including the partnership? _____
    a deputizing service? _____

17. How many outside lines are there? _____
    How many are available for incoming calls from patients? _____

Workload

Please enter the following statistics:

18. Number of patients seen by all doctors during one week:

	Mon.	Tues.	Wed.	Thurs.	Fri.	Sat.
Consulting a.m.						
Consulting p.m.						
Other special clinics						
New home visits						
Repeat home visits						

19. Number of patients seen by you during one week.

	Mon.	Tues.	Wed.	Thurs.	Fri.	Sat.
Consulting a.m.						
Consulting p.m.						
Other special clinics						
New home visits						
Repeat home visits						

20. Number of night visits in last full quarter done by practice _____

21. Special sessions: please specify number of hours per week:

Antenatal _____

Child health _____

Immunization _____

Family planning _____

Cervical cytology _____

Hypertension _____

Geriatric _____

Other _____

Staff

22. Staff employed: please list their names, duties and hours worked, so that they can be identified by the visitors.

Name	Duties	Hours worked

23. Staff attached: please list their names, duties and hours worked, so that they can be identified by the visitors.

Name	Duties	Hours worked

24. Special equipment for diagnosis and treatment:

_____

_____

_____

25. Diagnostic facilities available within your district:

_____

_____

_____

26. Do you have access to obstetric beds? _____

27. How many confinements have you had during the last quarter:

a) In shared care? _____

b) In complete care? _____

Immunization rates

28. What is the percentage of children over the age of 2 years on your list who have completed their childhood immunizations? _____

How were these figures obtained?

_____

_____

29. Do you have an age/sex register? _____

Is it manual? _____

or computerized? _____

30. For what purpose is it used?

_____

_____

_____

31. Do you have a disease index? _____

32. If so, please describe and state for what purpose it is used:

_____

_____

_____

_____

33. Is there a system for issuing repeat prescriptions without the patient being seen? _____

34. If so, please describe your system and protocol for recall:

_____

_____

_____

Library

35. What books do you refer to regularly in the practice?

_____

_____

_____

_____

36. What arrangements are made for purchasing new books?

_____

_____

37. What new books have been purchased in the last
12 months?

_____

_____

38. What journals do you read regularly?

_____

_____

_____

Education and practice management

39. Have you or your partners carried out any audit or
examination of practice activities in the past 2 years?
If so, please give details:

_____

_____

40. What postgraduate courses have you attended in the
last 12 months?

_____

_____

41. Are regular meetings held:

between the partners? _____ with other staff? _____
If so, please give details:

_____

_____

_____

Patient participation

42. Does the practice have a mechanism for dealing with
'customer complaints' or promoting consumer

relations generally? _____

If so, please give details:

_____

_____

_____

_____

Development

43. Please describe below

a) recent development of the practice:

_____

_____

_____

b) aims for development in the next few years:

_____

_____

_____

_____

APPENDIX 4

Assessment grid for practice visit

Source of information	*Area of performance*			
	1. *Professional values*	2. *Accessibility*	3. *Clinical competence*	4. *Ability to communicate*
1. Practice profile	Audit, teaching, learning. Meetings with practice staff and health professionals. Mechanism for customer complaints. Evolution of the practice.	Adequate consulting hours. Undertakes home visiting. Personal availability. Shares in rota duty.	Record cards. Practice equipment. Special registers. Library. Attendance at courses. Access to laboratory, x-ray and beds.	Patients' groups. Hand-outs.
2. Observation of premises, equipment, organization	Helpful, discreet staff. Good morale. Decent waiting conditions.	Ancillary staff are helpful. Clear arrangements for obtaining the doctor or his deputy.	Adequate facilities for consulting and examining. Regular use of equipment.	Patients' enquiries handled effectively.
3. Discussion with ancillary staff (and other members of the health care team)	Appointments system applied flexibly. Staff contribute to the life of the practice. Discretion in revealing information to third parties.	Knowledge of procedures. Tolerant. Demonstrate their facilitative role. Have clear idea of the doctor's whereabouts.		Practice policies formulated in consultation with staff. Ready, informal access to the doctor.
4. Records	Records usable for teaching, audit, research. Confidentiality preserved.	Continuity of care by the individual doctor.	Adequate ordered entries. Retrievability. Special registers. Summary cards or special sheets for: drug treatment, diagnoses, repeat prescriptions.	Legible informative entries. Clear referral letters.
5. Video-taped consultations	Treats all patients with respect. Explores patient's ideas, concerns and expectations about the problem(s) and management. Supportively encourages patient to accept appropriate degree of responsibility for own health. Establishes or maintains relationship with patient which is helpful to the provision of care.	Makes appropriate use of time and resources in the consultation.	Adequately defines problems presented or revealed. Judicious use of relevant examinations and tests. Considers factors which may put patient at risk. Plans appropriate management of problem(s) with patient. Prescribes carefully and responsibly.	Informality, openness and involvement. True dialogue. Information given to patient in appropriate detail. Clear unambiguous follow-up arrangements.
6. Interview with doctor	Changes in the practice initiated by him. Plans for future development. How he has changed as doctor/teacher.	Confirms information from other sources.	Sound management plans for patient care. Conversant with current trends in general practice.	Articulate and coherent. Puts his case over well.

APPENDIX 5
Notes for the doctor to be visited

Preparation

The paper "What Sort of Doctor?" outlined a proposed procedure for assessing a general practitioner in the setting of his own practice. We have now conducted a number of pilot visits, and these notes are intended to describe some of the pitfalls and problems that have been identified in these early visits, and to assist future assessors in the conduct of their visits.

The purpose of the visit

The visit is intended as an educational exercise to provide the doctor with an assessment by his peers of his performance in the practice. The visitors will all be doctors who have experience of being visited themselves. The report will be confidential and sent only to the doctor who has been visited. A number of things need to be prepared before the visit.

Partners

While the intention of the visit is to assess the individual doctor, much of the information will come from the whole practice, and the visit itself involves all the practice members and staff.

It is essential that all your partners and staff understand and accept the purpose of the visit. The visiting assessors will wish to have time for discussion with both your attached and ancillary staff, and it is useful if a time can be agreed when this can be done.

Timetable

It is essential that the timetable for the visit is agreed with the practice beforehand. The observation of the practice premises, the way it functions, is best done at the beginning of the day, when the practice is busy. The observation of the premises, the discussion with staff and the inspection of the records will take at least two hours, but the visitors do not need to be accompanied by the doctor during this time. Reviewing the video-taped consultation and interviewing the doctor both take up to an hour, and it may be helpful for the visitors to have time on their own at the end of the visit to prepare their report. A specimen timetable might be as follows:

09.00 – 11.00	Observation of the practice premises and records
11.00 – 12.00	Discussion with ancillary staff, practice nurse and other members of the health care team
12.00 – 13.00	Video-tape review
13.00 – 14.00	Lunch with partners
14.00 – 15.00	Interview with doctor
15.00 – 1600	Preparation of report

This timetable may, of course, vary with the timetable of the practice and the availability of its members.

Practice profile

The visitors would also like you to prepare some information that they can study before the visit. Please will you complete the practice profile and send it to the visitors, together with the survey of 20 records of patients for whom you care, preferably chosen at random.

Video recording consultations in practice

It is important that the doctor to be recorded becomes familiar with the recording equipment that he has borrowed, so that anxiety about the equipment does not intrude into the consultation. When setting up the equipment in the consultation room the camera, recorder, microphone and wires should be as unobtrusive as possible, so that they remain unnoticed by both doctor and patient.

Camera position

Camera position is important. Often the confines of the consulting room mean that the choice is limited, but if it is possible to include the facial expressions of both doctor and patient this is an advantage. If a wide-angle lens is not obtainable it is possible to increase the field of vision of the camera by using a mirror – the camera is pointed into a mirror, so that it records a mirror image of the consultation. This also has the advantage of making the camera unobtrusive. If it is possible, the examination couch should be excluded from the field of view of the camera.

Lighting

With modern cameras it is not now necessary to have additional lighting, though better quality pictures are obtained if there is more light in the consulting room. It is possible to increase the total light in the consulting room without using spotlights, by increasing the wattage of the bulbs in the existing light sockets, or maybe by adding an additional light; however, if a bright light shines into the lens of the camera the automatic iris will close.

Sound

Most modern video cameras have a microphone on the camera, and sound level is controlled automatically – this means that the microphone is 15 feet or more away from the subjects, and the sound can be distorted. An extension microphone on the desk will produce better quality sound, but it is important not to put it directly on the desk, because the rustle of papers and movements of the desk are picked up.

Use of the monitor

If the camera is being positioned in the corner of the room, it may be difficult to check the focus and angle through the viewfinder, and it will be necessary to use the television monitor to look at the picture that is being recorded. Once the camera is in place, however, the television can be removed from the room.

Consent

The patients must consent to their consultations being recorded, and should not be placed under any pressure to agree – for example, by being asked by the doctor as they enter the room – and they must also understand and agree to the recording being seen by other doctors after the consultation. A specimen consent form is attached: this can be given to the patients by the receptionist when they enter the waiting room, and they will then have time to think about it and can hand the form back either to the receptionist or the doctor before the consultation begins. It is also helpful to explain to the receptionist what is going on and why.

Patient and doctor acceptability

Many doctors are apprehensive about having their consultations recorded, and fear that it will also adversely affect their patients. However, most doctors find that they soon become unaware of the camera, and that their patients largely ignore it.

Preparation for the practice visit

For the purpose of the visit you will need to record at least one surgery. It is also useful to make a list of the patients whose consultations have been recorded – their age, problem and either the length of the consultation or the position on the tape of its beginning and end. When the video tape is being discussed it is helpful to have the patients' records available for reference.

Practice profile

(The practice profile is included here – see Appendix 3.)

Survey of clinical records

Do your records contain the following details? (Answer Y, N, N/A)

	1	2	3	4	5	6	7	8	9	10	11	12	13	14	15	16	17	18	19	20	Total
1. Date of birth																					
2. Recent marital status																					
3. Recent occupation																					
4. Continuation cards in chronological order																					
5. Hospital reports in chronological order																					
6. Copies of referral letters																					
7. Record of continued medication																					
8. Preventive medicine appropriate for age																					
9. Completed summary sheet																					
10. Does the clinical record for the last consultation clearly show: a) history																					
b) clinical findings																					
c) statement of problem																					
d) treatment given																					
e) investigation ordered																					
f) information given to the patient																					

APPENDIX 6
Notes for the visitors

Introduction

The paper "What Sort of Doctor?" outlined a proposed procedure for assessing a general practitioner in the setting of his own practice. We have now conducted a number of pilot visits, and these notes are intended to describe some of the pitfalls and problems that have been identified in these early visits, and to assist future assessors in the conduct of their visits.

The purpose of the visit

The visit is intended as an educational exercise to provide the doctor with an assessment by his peers of his performance in the practice. The visitors will all be doctors who have experience of being visited themselves. The report will be confidential and sent only to the doctor who has been visited.

Partners

While the intention of the visit is to assess the individual doctor, many of the sources of information – for example, the records and the appointment system – belong to the whole practice, and the visit itself involves all the practice members and staff.

The doctor's partners may not be members of the College and, while having agreed to the visit's taking place, may be less keen to be assessed themselves. They will also feel an understandable pride in their own practice, and want their own contributions to the practice to be acknowledged.

The conduct of these visits may have an important effect on the way the partners see the work of the College, and it is important that visitors are courteous, sensitive to the partners' feelings and explain the purposes of the visit and their questioning quite clearly.

Timetable

It is essential that the timetable for the visit is agreed with the practice beforehand. The observation of the practice premises and the way it functions is best done at the beginning of the day, when the practice is busy. The observation of the premises, the discussion with the staff and the inspection of the records will take at least two hours, but the visitors do not need to be accompanied by the doctor during this time. Reviewing the video-taped consultation and interviewing the doctor both take up to an hour, and it may be helpful for the visitors to have time on their own at the end of the visit to prepare their report. A specimen timetable might be as follows:

09.00 – 11.00   Observation of the practice premises and records

11.00 – 12.00   Discussion with ancillary staff, practice nurse and other members of the health care team

12.00 – 13.00   Video-tape review

13.00 – 14.00   Lunch with partners

14.00 – 15.00   Interview with doctor

15.00 – 1600   Preparation of report

This timetable may, of course, vary with the timetable of the practice and the availability of its members.

The visiting assessors will also need to agree among themselves beforehand about their method of working and the way they intend to use their time.

Definitions of terminology

(a) *Areas of performance*

The four areas of performance review are:
1. Professional values
2. Accessibility
3. Clinical competence
4. Ability to communicate

(b) *Criteria*

These are statements of the elements of competence considered good practice within each area of performance, against which the assessments can be made.

(c) *Levels of performance*

The degree and frequency of achievement for each element of good practice.

While the judgement of what level of performance is acceptable practice may vary with the circumstances or norms of practice, the criteria, on the other hand, are constant.

(d) *Sources of information*

The proposed assessment uses six sources of information about the doctor's level of performance in practice:
1. Practice profile
2. Observation of the premises and organization
3. Discussion with practice staff an primary health care team
4. Records and registers
5. Video-taped consultations
6. Interview with the doctor.

Observation of practice premises and organization

During this phase the visitors will be able to observe both the premises and the way the practice is working at a busy time of day. Some of the features of the practice which can be observed at this time include:

Waiting room   Space, comfort and atmosphere
Notices and leaflets
Toilet facilities for patients

Desk	Accessibility and confidentiality for patients Attitude of staff to patients
Telephone	Number of lines Waiting time Arrangements for taking visits Arrangements for access to the doctor Arrangements for out-of-hours calls

Appointments	Booking rate
	Waiting time for:
	    a) a routine appointment
	    b) an urgent appointment
	    c) in the waiting room
	Arrangements for continuity of care

Office	Space Filing system Repeat prescription system Arrangements for visiting Age/sex register, disease and other registers, and their use System for smears, etc. Introduction to staff Facilities for typing – organization
Consulting room	Space Equipment Sound proofing
Common room	For doctors/staff? Library—books journals

Discussions with members of the health care team

Those involved could include the receptionist, secretary, telephonist, filing clerk, practice nurse, practice manager, health visitor, other attached paramedicals, general practitioner trainee, and partners.

'Discussion' may take the form of an informal talk among a group, a chat with an individual, or a fairly structured interview. The practice manager (or senior receptionist) is better interviewed alone, and possibly in a slightly more formal way than the rest of the staff.

The style adopted by the assessors should be conversational rather than interrogatory. When questions do have to be asked these should as far as possible flow naturally from the previous response. The atmosphere should be one in which it appears the assessor's interest is aroused (as indeed it should) and he desires an explanation, rather than that he is administering a check-list to determine pass/fail.

The object is to obtain insight both into staff attitudes and their aptitudes. Assessors should try to satisfy themselves about the following questions:

1. Is the staff structure such that each individual member of staff knows to whom to turn in case of difficulties? In particular is the role of the practice manager or senior receptionist clearly defined and understood by all the members of staff?

2. Do the staff give evidence of having been appropriately involved in the formulating of practice policies?

3. Is there a sufficient number of staff on duty to cope with peak periods?

4. Are staff aware of the practice boundaries, the practice policy concerning patients who move beyond those boundaries but wish to remain with the practice, and the procedure to be followed when persons living within the practice area wish to change their doctor from another practice to this doctor?

5. Are staff familiar with the geography of the practice, the provision of public transport, and the problems which individual patients may have in reaching the surgery in a given time?

6. Do the staff know how to contact urgently one or more of the doctors in the practice, at any time during the working day?

7. Are the staff aware of the arrangements for patients requesting help out of hours, and conversant with their own role?

8. Do the staff facilitate access to the doctor of the patient's choice within a reasonable time?

9. Do the staff give evidence of explaining patiently, and in an appropriate way, any alternative arrangement for the patient to be seen?

10. Are the staff aware of practice policy when a patient requests an urgent appointment; and do they give evidence that such a policy is carried out in a way which causes minimum distress to the patients?

11. In making appointments, particularly patient-initiated appointments, do the staff give some priority to the principle of continuity of care?

12. Are the staff aware of the practice policy in handling requests for home visits during working hours? Is their own room for independent decision-making clearly laid out? When appropriate, have they fast access to one of the doctors who may wish to talk directly to whoever is making the request?

13. Are the staff aware of the procedure for handling a request for advice by telephone, and can they make satisfactory arrangements for a patient to talk to a doctor within a reasonable period of time?

14. Do they give clear evidence that they see their role primarily as one which facilitates patient care? Do they exhibit tolerance of the eccentric, demanding and difficult patient, and flexibility in applying this policy to the needs of unique and sometimes idiosyncratic individuals?

15. Are they careful in revealing information about patients to third parties?

16. Do they understand what is expected of them, especially in relation to the doctor's task?

17. How do they see their role?

18. Is there any sense of pressure, tension or conflict?

19. Is there evidence of discontent, cynicism or resentment?

20. What is the state of morale?

21. What continuity is there among part-timers at change-over?

22. How effective are the arrangements for relaying messages?

Discussion with attached staff may give information about the accessibility of the doctor, the use made of the skills of members of the team and the importance placed on communication and teamwork. They can also be asked about developments in the practice, particularly in the fields of preventive medicine and the continuity of care of chronic illnesses, and their own involvement in these developments.

Much of this information will be found to overlap with that obtained under 'Observation of the practice premises and organization'. Indeed, discussion with staff may well take place during such observations and will provide an opportunity to confirm, and possibly fill out, information contained in the practice profile. The findings from the discussions will be the most relevant to the area of Accessibility, to some extent to Ability to Communicate and Professional Values, and hardly at all to Clinical competence. No attempt should be made to score the elements derived from this particular method until all the other methods have yielded their findings.

Clinical records

The doctor will have provided a summary of his analysis for 20 of his records. The visitors will also need to review a sample of the records to assess the following:

1. How valuable are the records for patient management, anticipatory care and audit?

2. What efforts are being made to improve the records?

3. What information do the records give about:
   a) Clinical management of problems, both acute and long-term?
   b) Anticipatory care, e.g. records of blood pressure, smoking history, smears and immunizations?

4. Is there an age-sex register and diagnostic index, and what use is made of them?

Video-taped consultations

Guidelines for playback and evaluation

1. Allow at least an hour of uninterrupted time for the viewing of the video-taped consultations.

2. Review at least four consultations, which should be as different as possible. A consultation with a child, a consultation for an acute problem with a young adult, a consultation for an acute problem with an older person, and a consultation for a chronic problem should all be viewed.

3. The attached list of questions may be used to evaluate each consultation by the visitors and by the doctor who is being assessed. Please remember to be very specific in answering these questions, noting behaviour which leads you to your conclusions.

4. Before viewing each consultation the visiting assessors should read the patient's notes, so that they have available to them the same written information as the doctor who is being assessed.

5. After the consultation is over, any outstanding matters of fact should be clarified briefly with the doctor. This should not take long, and only those most pressing details should be sought. These may include such matters as the dose of a prescription given, or the occupation of the patient. This is not an opportunity to start quizzing the doctor about the reasons for certain decisions that have been taken.

6. The doctor who is being assessed should first be invited to comment on those tasks achieved well in the consultation. There should then follow a general discussion of the doctor's strengths as revealed by the questions. The discussion of the doctor's strengths should be extensive.

7. The doctor who is being assessed should then be invited to comment on those aspects of the consultation which were not achieved, or which could have been done more effectively. He should be encouraged to state both the reasons why the task was not achieved and any possible ways in which he would want to improve his consultation. The visitors may then comment under the same heading, namely tasks which were not achieved and alternative suggestions. It is essential that alternatives are suggested, since without them the doctor may feel that he is merely being criticized.

It should always be borne in mind that the object of the practice visit is to share views with a colleague in a helpful way. Similarly it should also be remembered that a sample of four consultations is totally inadequate to review the full range of the doctor's skills and behaviour. Therefore emphasis should be placed on consistencies between all four consultations, rather than inconsistencies. If, for example, the assessors find that the doctor in question does not share management decisions with the patient in any of the four consultations, this is much more significant than an occasional lapse. It is also possible to see from these guidelines that the review of video-taped consultations can only take place in the presence of the doctor who has performed them. The importance of handling sensitively this particular interview with the doctor cannot be over-emphasized.

Seven questions to ask about each consultation

1. How completely did the doctor find out why the patient came? In order to do this the doctor will probably have had to explore:
   (a) the nature and history of the patient's problems
   (b) the aetiology of the problem
   (c) the patient's ideas, concerns and expectations about the problems and their management
   (d) the effects of the problems.

2. Did the doctor consider other possible problems this patient might be facing, including:
   (a) continuing problems
   (b) at risk factors?

3. To what extent did the doctor choose *with the patient* an appropriate action for each problem presented or revealed?

4. To what extent did the doctor achieve a shared understanding of the problems with the patient?

5. To what extent did the doctor involve the patient in the management of the problems and encourage the patient to accept an appropriate degree of responsibility for their management?

6. To what extent did the doctor use time and other resources appropriately both in the consultation and in the long term?

7. To what extent did the doctor establish or maintain a relationship with the patient which helped them both to achieve all of these tasks?

Interview with the doctor

The purpose of the interview with the doctor being visited is to clarify or expand upon information gleaned earlier on, and "to elicit his views and understanding on a variety of topics".

In order to be effective the interview should include some examination with the doctor of all areas where apparent problems have been identified. The dangers therefore range from the interview being too threatening a procedure on the one hand, to simply being a 'cosy chat', involving collusion to avoid sensitive areas, on the other. This method of assessment should be sensitively handled if "What Sort of Doctor?" is to be widely acceptable. The following suggestions may be helpful:

1. The interview should be the final session of the visit, and be allowed adequate time.

2. The visiting team should include at least one assessor with experience of visiting, and a practitioner from the local faculty. It would be valuable if after completing the assessment the two assessors could evaluate the visit itself, and discover the host doctor's observations on the experience.

3. Early experience suggests that doctors being visited (and indeed their partners) can be irritated by the interview. This is most likely to happen if topics outside the agreed criteria are discussed (e.g. financial arrangements within the practice), or if the personal opinions of the visitors are expressed in their report. It is suggested that throughout the visit and the report the assessors adhere to the criteria defined in the "What Sort of Doctor?" document.

4. In examining the doctor's working methods with him, judgemental attitudes are avoided if a range of alternative methods of tackling the same problem is discussed, thereby increasing the educational value of the interview.

5. In order to emphasize the two-way educational process during the interview the doctor could be encouraged to spend a little time stating his views on the most positive achievements of his practice (i.e. what he feels he does well).

6. The visitors should remember the statement in the "What Sort of Doctor?" document (paragraph 25):

   "The undoubted tensions experienced by the host doctor have to a large extent been mitigated by the familiarity, friendly rivalry and the sense of a common task."

If we strive for these attributes during our visits we can increase the acceptability of the "What Sort of Doctor?" exercise throughout the faculties.

Report on the practice visit

Each method of assessment is a source of information in each of the four areas of performance. During the visit it may be helpful to use the assessment grid as an *aide mémoire*.

A written report should be provided, based on the criteria in the four areas of performance. It should always include a factual statement of the evidence on which the assessment has been made, and care should be taken to give full weight first to the strengths that have been observed, while any criticisms made should be coupled with recommendations or suggestions of alternative options.

The report should be sent only to the doctor who has been visited, who may show it to other members of the practice or not, as he chooses. Care should be taken with the writing of the report, but it is important to let the doctor have it as soon as it is available.

Outline grid for practice visit

Method	Area of performance			
	1. *Professional values*	2. *Accessibility*	3. *Clinical competence*	4. *Ability to communicate*
1. Practice profile				
2. Premises and organization				
3. Discussion with staff				
4. Records				
5. Video-taped consultations				
6. Interview with doctor				

APPENDIX 7
Sample results of a visit

Report on the assessment visit

Dr A. is in general practice with two partners in X, a village with a population of 5,000. He has been there for 20 years and was joined by Dr B. in 1970 and Dr C. more recently. With relatively small average lists the accent of the practice is on quality of care rather than coping with a large demand, and each partner has a day off in the week.

The practice premises are purpose built with plenty of room for an increase in practice size in the future. Considerable thought had obviously gone into the original design by Dr A., which resulted in a single-storey building with plenty of light, reasonably sized consulting rooms and main office, large treatment room, and rooms for the health visitor and secretary.

Dr A. sent copies of his informative practice profile, together with a road map showing the location of the practice, to us before the visit. We were able to see the practice in action on a quiet day, meet the ancillary and attached staff, and have lunch with the partners. The whole atmosphere was one of welcoming friendliness.

1. *Professional values*

Dr A. is a thoughtful and caring general practitioner, concerned to treat the patient as a whole and this was shown in several ways. His own particular interests have led him to take part in Balint seminars for several years, to learn about hypnotism and homœopathy and use them in his practice, and more recently to join the holistic medicine movement. He has run a hypertension clinic for many years, and more recently started a well woman clinic with an effective recall system, staffed by a nurse. The close working relationship with nurse, midwife and health visitor apparent when we interviewed them added to the impression that a full and comprehensive service was being offered to the patient. However, although the treatment room is used for various clinics, no attempt is made to offer a 'casualty' or 'minor op' service and it was not equipped for this. Care is extended into the community and there are regular meetings with clergy and the headmaster of the secondary school to discuss local problems such as adolescent vandalism.

The partnership does not attempt to operate a personal list system although most patients do in fact usually see the same doctor. There is a strong sense of practice development, with several innovations, such as the well woman clinic. The partners discussed easily together the likely growth of the practice and their own attitudes and new ideas. Dr A.'s bookshelf, his video consultations and his interview all confirmed his enthusiastic desires to develop personal skills to help his patients in all ways possible.

Although he had not had much opportunity to see his consultation on video before, he willingly entered the spirit of the "What Sort of Doctor?" assessment and was openly introspective. His apostolic view is that patients should be enabled to adopt solutions to problems for themselves, but he shows signs of directing patients into this attitude rather than enabling them to adopt it. Use of video in his local trainers' workshop, and for teaching his own trainee, might help him to achieve the high standard which he sets for his own consultations.

Dr A. had his trainee with him on the day of our visit and a relaxed and co-operative relationship was apparent between them. He is a past course organizer and although he scored himself low for teaching and research in his own assessment, he has several interesting innovations in his own practice. He is a well respected, thoroughly professional doctor, who seeks to maintain high standards of medicine and improve his service to his patients.

2. *Accessibility*

There is an appointments system, the three partners offering adequate consulting time so that all patients can be given an appointment on the day they wish, usually with their own doctor. Home visits are also carried out on the day requested, and seemed few in number, probably because of the small list size and well defined, relatively small practice area. Dr A. felt that routine follow-up visiting of the elderly has little value, but his partner undertakes this.

The receptionist understood completely the procedures for making appointments, dealing with repeat prescriptions, contacting the doctors for out-of-hours calls. These are taken by the doctor on duty for the day and night. There has been no difficulty in contacting the doctor on call, but as the partners live some way from the surgery a radio-pager might be of help.

Patients are able to see the community nurse, midwife and health visitor at the practice and are encouraged to do so when it seems appropriate.

Patients are called to the consulting room by a buzzer, but the waiting room cannot be seen from the reception area, and this could cause problems at times.

The practice has recently appointed a full-time secretary who deals with letters and FPC work. Her office is small but adequate with a particularly useful storage file. Lack of a telephone extension in her room might lead to inefficiencies.

Generally, the practice is organized to give maximum accessibility for the patients to the doctor. However, we thought that the partners had not looked at the effect that this policy of open access and one day off a week had on continuity of personal care: whether this matters or not in a small practice is a most interesting point!

3. *Clinical competence*

The clinical competence of the practice, in the widest sense, is excellent. There is a high immunization and cervical cytology take-up. Full obstetric care is available either in the local maternity unit, or at home, for suitable cases, backed up by an enthusiastic and experienced midwife. The partners do not necessarily go to all deliveries at the general practitioner unit, and this is understandable because of the distance involved, but it might lead to a problem with fetal distress or other complications of confinement. A high level of clinical competence in management of patients was apparent in the cases studied and the videos, but was not perhaps always reflected in the notes made at the time, which were rather sketchy and incomplete. It might be difficult for a partner or trainee to follow his management from the note written. His interviewing technique on the video suggested a relaxed and caring attitude with good fact-finding and careful examination when appropriate. The flow of the consultation was good, although sometimes interrupted by note writing, which could be left to the end.

The explanations given to patients were full and attempted to deal with the whole problem with the patient involved in decision and management. In the interviews we saw it seemed that time might have been saved by first discovering the patient's understanding of the problem, then the doctor enlarging on this. Dr A. does not feel that minor surgery, or the use of an ECG machine, would have much place in his practice. He is most interested in those areas of medicine which are highly relevant to general practice and which involve counselling and encouraging self-reliance, and actively seeks to improve his knowledge and skills in these areas.

4. *Ability to communicate*

The relaxed and helpful reception, early appointments, thoughtfully furnished consulting room, with a child's play area and a clear desk, together with Dr A.'s friendly manner, all foster good communication with the patients. In the consultations seen, he gave his patients his undivided attention except when writing notes, and generally listened to what they said without undue interruption. His ability to communicate well is seen also in his good relationships with his partners, apparent at the lunchtime meeting when they were able to talk freely about patients' behaviour towards them. The midwife, community nurse and health visitor all felt that they could easily approach Dr A. about problems.

The age-sex and household registers are maintained in an efficient way by a part-time secretary who also organizes all records coming into the practice. All the records we looked at were in chronological order and some had summary cards. There is a monthly practice meeting which is well attended, when 'hot' problems, special topics or changes in the practice are discussed. Referral letters are typewritten and contain all relevant information, and copies are filed.

Summary

Dr A. is a keen practitioner who has developed his practice to suit his own interests (e.g. holistic medicine, counselling, and hypnotherapy). In no way does he impede his partners in developing theirs; indeed, he may spur them on. His meticulous nature is reflected in the well kept records, design of the surgery and attention to detail in his room arrangement. This has led to a practice that has areas which, from the patients' point of view, might be improved.

1. Under-use of large treatment room: casualties presumably go to neighbouring hospitals.

2. Under-use of ECG machine: policy with regard to coronary heart care not clear.

3. Difficulty in contacting doctor on call in an emergency.

4. Intranatal care undertaken (what a relief to see it), but we were a little uneasy about cover of 'flat' babies.

5. Note-taking could be improved.

Despite these comments, this practice and doctor are well ahead of the field.

Comments by the assessor

1. *Practice profile*
This was very fully filled in: a useful introduction to the practice and 'prompt' for visit and report writing.

2. *Premises and organization*
It was useful to see the premises being used on day of visit. The organization was difficult to judge as a visit is bound to be a 'special' day.

3. *Interview with staff*
All the staff were very helpful and willing to spend time describing their role in practice and answering questions.

4. *Records and registers*
The registers were good and well presented. We did not spend enough time looking at the *content* of the notes; this can give good information about case management.

Comments by the doctor visited

Soon after the visit

1. The practice profile should have a box to indicate the number of patients having maternity care in the practice.

2. I thought the assessment was fair and thorough.

3. The visit was valuable. The main change is an acceleration in the filling in of summary of treatment cards. We had already been assessing the value of database cards. These have now arrived and are being given to new patients and adult previous patients.

4. My patients and staff seemed to be interested in the visit and enjoyed talking about themselves and their work.

5. In my own visits I felt that I was short of time. As we only have a single surgery it seemed that there was adequate time available. The assessors did not leave the surgery till about 4.30 p.m.

Made some time later

1. *Medical records.* The visit has been effective in giving us fresh impetus in producing summary cards for a greater proportion of the patients than before. We have also acquired database cards which are given to all new patients. Our receptionists have been very resistant to giving them to all patients and manage to forget to give them out to the patients when they are at the reception desk. These cards should be taken away by the patient, filled in and returned as soon as possible to be placed in their medical records. We have just spent a considerable amount of money on buying a carousel which should hold about two thousand records, thus relieving some of the pressure on our open-topped shelving.

2. *Communication.* We meet for lunch more often than previously and there is much better communication between the partners and the trainee with a discussion of problems.

3. *Equipment.* We have studied the use of radio telephones and because most patients' records carry their telephone number we have considered this unnecessary. We have tested for a week some dictation and transcribing equipment but feel that this particular model was too expensive. I hope to find more acceptable cheaper equipment.

4. *Personal growth.* It is difficult to be objective about this. I have been pushing for our postgraduate centre to purchase a video camera for use in our surgery. This has been agreed in principle and it will be available soon. We will be assessing the recordings in the trainers' workshop.

A SYSTEM OF TRAINING
FOR GENERAL PRACTICE

Occasional Paper 4

The Department of General Practice at the University of Exeter was the first Department of General Practice in Europe to be set up outside an undergraduate medical school and it has since its inception concentrated particularly on vocational training for general practice.

Occasional Paper 4, written by Dr D. J. Pereira Gray, Senior lecturer in-Charge, presents clear statements of this Department's philosophy and aims, and outlines one practical method of organizing three years of specific training for general medical practice.

A System of Training for General Practice, Occasional Paper 4, can be obtained from the Publications Sales Office, Royal College of General Practitioners, 8 Queen Street, Edinburgh EH2 1JE, price £3.00 including postage. Payment should be made with order.

SOME AIMS OF TRAINING
FOR GENERAL PRACTICE

Occasional Paper 6

The Royal College of General Practitioners has now agreed three sets of educational objectives for doctors training for general practice: the first on child care with the British Paediatric Association, the second on the care of the elderly with the British Geriatric Society, and the third on the care of the mentally ill with the Royal College of Psychiatrists.

The booklet also contains the job definition and educational aims for general practice as a whole which have been agreed by the Leeuwenhorst Working Party and approved by the Royal College of General Practitioners.

Some Aims of Training for General Practice, Occasional Paper 6, can be obtained from the Publications Sales Office, Royal College of General Practitioners, 8 Queen Street, Edinburgh EH2 1JE, price £2.75 including postage. Payment should be made with order.

SECTION 63 ACTIVITIES

Occasional Paper 11

Much of the continuing education provided for general practice through the National Health Service and the vast majority of vocational training as well is financed under Section 63.

What sort of educational activities are provided? How logical is the basis for all this work, and what are the views of the doctors concerned with providing lectures? How effective anyway is all this education? These, and many other controversial topics are tackled by Mrs Jo Wood and the late Professor P. S. Byrne from the Department of General Practice at the University of Manchester, which has an international reputation for its reports on medical education with reference to general practice.

Section 63 Activities, Occasional Paper 11, can be obtained from the Publications Sales Office, Royal College of General Practitioners, 8 Queen Street, Edinburgh EH2 1JE, price £3.75 including postage. Payment should be made with order.

FOURTH NATIONAL TRAINEE
CONFERENCE
REPORT, RECOMMENDATIONS
AND QUESTIONNAIRE

Occasional Paper 18

How much teaching do vocational trainees really get? What do they think about their trainers and how easily can they talk to them? This *Occasional Paper* reports on the proceedings of the Fourth National Trainee Conference held at Exeter in July 1980 and analyses the results of a questionnaire which was returned by 1,680 trainees throughout the country.

This is the most detailed information so far published about the opinions of trainees, and from them a new 'value for money' index has been derived, based on sophisticated statistical analysis, which now makes it possible for the first time to rate a general practitioner trainer.

Fourth National Trainee Conference, Occasional Paper 18, can be obtained from the Publications Sales Office, Royal College of General Practitioners, 8 Queen Street, Edinburgh EH2 1JE, price £3.75 including postage. Payment should be made with order.

THE INFLUENCE OF TRAINERS ON TRAINEES IN GENERAL PRACTICE

Occasional Paper 21

This *Occasional Paper* on vocational training reports on the educational progress of a group of trainees in the North of England. Two groups of trainees were identified (those who underwent the greatest change and those who underwent the least change precourse to postcourse) and their characteristics were compared with the characteristics of their trainers. This is the first time this has been done and several new findings have emerged.

The findings are fully consistent with those of *Occasional Paper 18* and add still further support for the present system of selecting training practices. The report will therefore need to be considered by regional general practice subcommittees, course organizers, and regional advisers, and is recommended to all trainers and trainees.

The Influence of Trainers on Trainees in General Practice, Occasional Paper 21, can be obtained from the Publications Sales Office, Royal College of General Practitioners, 8 Queen Street, Edinburgh EH2 1JE, price £3.25 including postage. Payment should be made with order.

UNDERGRADUATE MEDICAL EDUCATION IN GENERAL PRACTICE

Occasional Paper 28

The General Medical Council is responsible for giving guidance to all medical schools about the content of courses leading to medical qualifications. Its recommendations are in fact much more clear and specific than is generally known and many highlight quite unambiguously the need for medical students to learn from general practice.

A working group of the Association of University Teachers in General Practice has studied the recommendations in detail and analysed the special contribution which general practice can play in meeting the GMC recommendations. Their comments will be invaluable in furthering discussions about departments of general practice in many universities.

Undergraduate Medical Education in General Practice, Occasional Paper 28, can be obtained from the Publications Sales Office, Royal College of General Practitioners, 8 Queen Street, Edinburgh EH2 1JE, price £3.50 including postage. Payment should be made with order.

TRAINEE PROJECTS

Occasional Paper 29

What subjects are suitable for trainee projects? Do many get published? How should a research protocol be constructed and what are the characteristics of trainees who complete projects?

These and other topics are considered in *Trainee Projects, Occasional Paper 29,* which not only gives examples of actual projects (three prize-winning essays in the National Syntex Award scheme and nearly 50 summaries of local award-winning papers) but also includes advice from Professor J. G. R. Howie on constructing a research protocol, Dr D. J. Pereira Gray on encouraging project work, and Dr Michael Mead who writes from experience of carrying out projects as a trainee.

Trainee Projects, Occasional Paper 29, can be obtained from the Publications Sales Office, Royal College of General Practitiners, 8 Queen Street, Edinburgh EH2 1JE, price £4.50 including postage. Payment should be made with order.

PRIORITY OBJECTIVES FOR GENERAL PRACTICE VOCATIONAL TRAINING

Occasional Paper 30

One of the biggest problems in vocational training for general practice has been the need to design courses appropriate for doctors preparing to work in the widest of all medical roles. The need is to decide what subjects are important and what priority objectives should be.

This *Occasional Paper* comes from the Course Organizers and Regional Advisers Group in the Oxford Region, which has a distinguished record in developing vocational training. Based on widespread consultation within the Region, the group achieved a consensus on its priorities, which it lists under five headings: primary care, communication, organization, professional values, and personal and professional growth. It therefore provides a useful basis for discussion in other regions.

Priority Objectives for General Practice Vocational Training, Occasional Paper 30, is available from the Publications Sales Office, Royal College of General Practitioners, 8 Queen Street, Edinburgh EH2 1JE, price £3.50, including postage. Payment should be made with order.

THE FUTURE GENERAL PRACTITIONER—LEARNING AND TEACHING

This book has become the best selling of the Royal College of General Practitioners' books. Since it was first published in 1972, it has been reprinted several times and translated into four different languages.

Its classification of the content of general practice/family medicine has since been used throughout the English-speaking world.

The Future General Practitioner—Learning and Teaching is available now from the Publications Sales Office, Royal College of General Practitioners, 8 Queen Street, Edinburgh EH2 1JE, price £10.50 or £9.50 for members of the College. Prices include postage. Payment should be made with order.

A HISTORY OF THE ROYAL COLLEGE OF GENERAL PRACTITIONERS

This book records early attempts to form a College, the birth of the College itself, and the story of its growth through childhood to maturity. Edited by three distinguished founder members, John Fry, Lord Hunt of Fawley and R. J. F. H. Pinsent, it is a fascinating tribute to the enthusiasm, persistence and dedication of the men who made the College.

Written by those who were actually involved, the chapters describe not only the development of the organization of the College as a whole but of each of its component parts. Thus its involvement with medical education, standards, research and literature is described as well as its relationships with other bodies at home and abroad.

A History of the Royal College of General Practitioners can be obtained from the Publications Sales Office, Royal College of General Practitioners, 8 Queen Street, Edinburgh EH2 1JE, price £10 to members, £12 to non-members, including postage. Payment should be made with order.

PRESENT STATE AND FUTURE NEEDS IN GENERAL PRACTICE

The sixth edition of this well known book by John Fry gives numerous facts and figures about general practice and is a basic reference for all those interested in primary medical care.

Dr Fry has again summarized key information such as the average number of patients, patterns of allowances, and numbers of trainers and teaching practices in a series of tables and charts, supported by a clear commentary. Particularly useful is the conversion of current rates for illness and services in relation to population units of 2,500 (about one general practitioner) and 10,000 (a typical group practice).

Present State and Future Needs in General Practice has been published for the College by MTP Press Limited and is available from the Publications Sales Office, Royal College of General Practitioners, 8 Queen Street, Edinburgh EH2 1JE, price £5.50, including postage. Payment should be made with order.

HANDBOOK OF PREVENTIVE CARE FOR PRE-SCHOOL CHILDREN

Children form about a quarter of the population and good preventive care can save substantial disabilities. The General Medical Services Committee and the Royal College of General Practitioners have jointly published a handbook for preventive care of pre-school children and have also designed record cards for use in general practice which fit both Lloyd George envelopes and A4 folders.

Good preventive care for children is becoming one of the hallmarks of modern general practice and this handbook sets out clearly and simply what should be done and why.

The *Handbook of Preventive Care for Pre-school Children* is available with two sample record cards, price £1.00 including postage, from the Information Service, Royal College of General Practitioners, 14 Princes Gate, Hyde Park, London SW7 1PU. The cards are also available separately from the same address at a cost of £3.00 per 100 for those fitting the Lloyd George envelopes and £8.50 per 100 for size A4. Postage and packing costs for all cards are as follows: 100: £2.50; 200: £3.00; 300: £5.00; 400: £5.00; 500: £7.50.

WILLIAM PICKLES

William Pickles was one of the outstanding general practitioners of our time. His *Epidemiology in Country Practice*, first published in 1939, was reprinted by the College in 1972 but has not been available for some years. Similarly his biography *Will Pickles of Wensleydale* by Professor John Pemberton, who was both a friend and colleague, has also been out of print for some time.

The College has now republished both books simultaneously. *Epidemiology in Country Practice* is a classic example of original research in general practice and *Will Pickles of Wensleydale* is the definitive biography of Pickles written in a pleasing and easy-to-read style. These two books, which both separately and together contribute to the history of general practice, can be warmly recommended.

The books are available from the Publications Sales Office, Royal College of General Practitioners, 8 Queen Street, Edinburgh EH2 1JE. *Epidemiology in Country Practice* is £5.50, *Will Pickles of Wensleydale* is £10.50; if ordered together the two books can be bought at the reduced price of £13.00. All prices include postage, and payment should be made with order.

DOCTORS TALKING TO PATIENTS

Doctors Talking to Patients, by Professor P. S. Byrne, a distinguished past-President of the Royal College of General Practitioners, and Dr B. E. L. Long, an expert educationalist, was first published by HMSO in 1976.

This well-known book has made a major contribution to the understanding of the consultation in general practice and illustrates the potential for using modern methods of recording for analysing the problems of doctor-patient communication.

With permission of HMSO, the Royal College of General Practitioners has now reprinted *Doctors Talking to Patients* and so made available this classic work to a new generation of trainees and general practitioner principals.

Doctors Talking to Patients can be obtained from the Publications Sales Office, Royal College of General Practitioners, 8 Queen Street, Edinburgh EH2 1JE, price £10.50 including postage. Payment should be made with order.

COMBINED REPORTS ON PREVENTION

Reports from General Practice 18–21

The College's campaign for health promotion and disease prevention in general practice was signalled by the publication in the years 1981–82 of a series of documents on different aspects of preventive medicine in general practice.

Although at the time these were distributed free of charge with the *Journal* to all Fellows, Members and Associates of the College, the steady demand for these documents has led to several of them going out of print.

Combined Reports on Prevention thus brings together between one set of covers *Reports from General Practice 18, 19, 20 and 21*, which deal with the principles of prevention, prevention of arterial disease, prevention of psychiatric disorders, and family planning.

The combined reports can be obtained from the Publications Sales Office, Royal College of General Practitioners, 8 Queen Street, Edinburgh EH2 1JE, price £4.50 including postage. Payment should be made with order.

HEALTHIER CHILDREN— THINKING PREVENTION

Report from General Practice 22

The care of children is one of the most important and most rapidly developing aspects of modern general practice. *Healthier Children—Thinking Prevention* describes in detail the general principles which govern the care of children within the framework of family practice.

The report includes detailed schedules of examinations appropriate to the primary health care team, analyses of doctor/patient relationships, teamwork, and principles of remuneration and decribes a number of new ideas on monitoring. Ideas for training are also discussed, both for doctors and other health professionals, and new evidence is presented to show why general practice is now ready to undertake the health surveillance of children.

Healthier Children—Thinking Prevention, Report from General Practice 22, is available from the Publications Sales Office, Royal College of General Practitioners, 8 Queen Street, Edinburgh EH2 1JE, price £5.50 including postage. Payment should be made with order.

COMPUTERS IN PRIMARY CARE

Occasional Paper 13

Computers are coming. More and more general practitioners are computerizing aspects of their record systems in general medical practice.

Computers in Primary Care is the report of a working party of the Royal College of General Practitioners which describes the possibilities currently available and looks into the future, discussing both technical and financial aspects.

The members of this working party have between them considerable experience of using computers in general practice. Together they summarize the experience and philosophy which they have acquired which enables them to put forward a series of conclusions and recommendations for the future.

Computers in Primary Care, Occasional Paper 13, was reprinted in 1982, and can be obtained from the Publications Sales Office, Royal College of General Practitioners, 8 Queen Street, Edinburgh EH2 1JE, price £3.00 including postage. Payment should be made with order.

THE MEASUREMENT OF THE QUALITY OF GENERAL PRACTITIONER CARE

Occasional Paper 15

The race to measure the quality of care in general practice is on, and the promotion of quality is one of the main objectives of the Royal College of General Practitioners. Nevertheless, for many years the identification of criteria of quality has proved elusive.

Occasional Paper 15 is a detailed review of the literature by Dr C. J. Watkins, one of the senior lecturers in general practice at St Thomas' Hospital Medical School, and forms part of the work for which he was subsequently awarded a PhD. It is therefore essential reading for those who are studying this fascinating subject.

The Measurement of the Quality of General Practitioner Care, Occasional Paper 15, can be obtained from the Publications Sales Office, Royal College of General Practitioners, 8 Queen Street, Edinburgh EH2 1JE, price £3.00 including postage. Payment should be made with order.

BOOKING FOR MATERNITY CARE A COMPARISON OF TWO SYSTEMS

Occasional Paper 31

Do women care where their babies are delivered? Can the differences they experience in two different systems of care be measured?

Professor Michael Klein, from a Department of General Practice in Canada, and Ms Diana Elbourne, from the National Perinatal Epidemiology Unit in Oxford, used research material gathered in Oxford to carry out a detailed study of the views of mothers booked for delivery in a general practitioner unit and those booked for shared care in a specialist consultant unit. The findings are of considerable interest particularly in relation to women booked for general practitioner care. The study thus contributes to the continuing debate about the appropriate place of general practitioner obstetrics in a modern health system.

Booking for Maternity Care – A Comparison of Two Systems, Occasional Paper 31, can be obtained from the Publications Sales Office, Royal College of General Practitioners, 8 Queen Street, Edinburgh EH2 1JE, price £3.50 including postage. Payment should be made with order.

PROMOTING PREVENTION

Occasional Paper 22

In 1981 and 1982 the College published five *Reports from General Practice* from five sub-committees of its Working Party on Prevention. These dealt with the principles of prevention, the prevention of arterial disease, the prevention of psychiatric disorders, family planning, and child health, all in relation to general practice.

The reports initiated a major debate on the place of prevention in health care. Now another working party has produced a discussion document which pulls together the threads of the five reports and identifies practical ways in which their recommendations might be implemented. Implementation, if carried out, would involve many bodies and organizations and have a major impact on health care.

Promoting Prevention, Occasional Paper 22, can be obtained from the Publications Sales Office, Royal College of General Practitioners, 8 Queen Street, Edinburgh EH2 1JE, price £3.00 including postage. Payment should be made with order.

PRESCRIBING—
A SUITABLE CASE FOR TREATMENT

Occasional Paper 24

General practitioner prescribing continues to attract attention, both in relation to quality and to costs. Quality concerns safety, relevance and effectiveness, while the cost of the average general practitioner's prescriptions now exceeds the cost of his income and expenses combined.

Prescribing—A Suitable Case for Treatment reports a study which examined both these factors. Prescriptions returned from the Prescription Pricing Authority were used to analyse the prescribing of a study group and of a group of matched controls; this was backed up by an educational programme involving discussions between members of the study group. The results suggest that with this kind of encouragement practitioners could reduce both the level and the cost of their prescribing.

Prescribing—A Suitable Case for Treatment, Occasional Paper 24, can be obtained from the Publications Sales Office, Royal College of General Practitioners, 8 Queen Street, Edinburgh EH2 1JE, price £3.75 including postage. Payment should be made with order.

SOCIAL CLASS AND HEALTH STATUS:
INEQUALITY OR DIFFERENCE

Occasional Paper 25

It is known that social class is a major determinant of health and death: what is not clear is how general practitioners respond to illness presented by patients in different social classes. Although the Black Report was unconvinced about differential response, Dr Donald Crombie in his important McConaghey Memorial Lecture provides new evidence that general practitioners actively compensate by providing more consultations and more care for patients in social classes 4 and 5.

This lecture gives factual evidence and provides striking tables showing that the variations of care between general practitioners is now greater than variations due to patient factors such as age, sex and social class; in other words the doctor is the most important variable in general practice.

Social Class and Health Status, Occasional Paper 25, can be obtained from the Publications Sales Office, Royal College of General Practitioners, 8 Queen Street, Edinburgh EH2 1JE, price £3.50 including postage. Payment should be made with order.

CLASSIFICATION OF DISEASES,
PROBLEMS AND PROCEDURES 1984

Occasional Paper 26

The new College classification of health problems from the Manchester Research Unit of the Royal College of General Practitioners is a major academic event. This is the first time that the old College classification has been blended thoroughly with the *International Classification of Disease* and that it has been made available in both electronic and printed form.

The printed version, published as *Occasional Paper 26*, describes the background of the classification, offers guidance on its use, and gives the classification in full, first in code order and then in alphabetical groups.

Approved by the Council of the College in 1983, this is likely to be the definitive text on classification in general practice for many years.

Classification of Diseases, Problems and Procedures 1984, Occasional Paper 26, can be obtained from the Publications Sales Office, Royal College of General Practitioners, 8 Queen Street, Edinburgh EH2 1JE, price £4.75 including postage. Payment should be made with order.

CLINICAL KNOWLEDGE AND
EDUCATION FOR GENERAL PRACTICE

Occasional Paper 27

How do general practitioners care for common clinical conditions? How much are they influenced by what they know and what they don't know? Are trainers any different and what would consultants feel about these clinical standards anyway? These and other controversial subjects have been tackled by Dr H. W. K. Acheson of the Department of General Practice, University of Manchester.

In a study carried out by postal questionnaire, Dr Acheson asked groups of practitioners what action they would take in relation to seven common clincial conditions and as a yardstick asked the same questions of groups of consultants in the specialties concerned. The answers are not only thought-provoking in themselves but have implications for undergraduate, vocational, and continuing education for general practice.

Clinical Knowledge and Education for General Practice, Occasional Paper 27, can be obtained from the Publications Sales Office, Royal College of General Practitioners, 8 Queen Street, Edinburgh EH2 1JE, price £3.50 including postage. Payment should be made with order.

PROGRESS
IN · THE · SERVICE · OF · MEDICINE

Stuart Pharmaceuticals Limited is a subsidiary of ICI, contributing to the ICI Pharmaceuticals Group investment of over £100 million (1985) in original Research and Development.

Stuart believes in a partnership with the medical professions and offers many services to medical education and practice management.

Just some examples of these are a free aneroid sphygmomanometer testing service, 'Heartbeat' – a remarkable interactive video disc programme, and the recently introduced "Stuart Reception Review".

These services complement Stuart's product range, which centres around cardiovascular medicines, and together they are backed by a team of responsible and thoroughly trained staff. Many of these key components of Stuart appear below.

STUART

Stuart Pharmaceuticals Limited,
Stuart House,
50 Alderley Road,
Wilmslow
Cheshire SK9 1RE